T.D. JAKES

Presented To:

_____

_____

From:

_____

_____

Date:

_____

_____

Loose That Man
and
Let Him Go!

DEVOTIONAL

Loose That Man and Let Him Go!

Devotional

So You Call Yourself a Man?

by T. D. Jakes

ALBURY PUBLISHING
Tulsa, Oklahoma

Unless otherwise indicated, all Scripture quotations are taken from the *King James Version* of the Bible.

Loose That Man and Let Him Go! Devotional
So You Call Yourself a Man?

ISBN 1-57778-086-8

Copyright © 1998 by
T. D. Jakes
P. O. 210887
Dallas, Texas 75211

Published by ALBURY PUBLISHING
P. O. Box 470406
Tulsa, Oklahoma 74147-0406

TO

my sons who are in the process of becoming
men of integrity.

I, like most parents, am full of hopes and dreams
loaded with rather lofty expectations of grandeur.
Nevertheless, should my sons fall short of my hopes,
I will remain faithful to my call — the call to be
their father. It is not a position to be resigned but a
relationship to be relied upon. It is a call I am glad
to fulfill as with all men who have someone
who believes in them.

The world awaits you!

CONTENTS

Introduction

Time for a New Level of Reconciliation and Healing!

"And they sung a new song, saying, Thou art worthy . . . for thou wast slain, and hast redeemed us to God by thy blood out of every kindred, and tongue, and people, and nation" (Revelation 5:9).

The church that I pastor is multiracial and multicultural. I believe that is part of God's plan for reconciliation in these last days. I don't believe you can have multiplication if you only have duplication of like elements. Multiplication is born of reconciliation among those with differences.

God loves a multiplicity of people and He blesses people in a multiplicity of ways. We must be willing to accept the different ways in which people receive blessings and then thank God for them. We must be willing to accept different ways of worshiping the Lord Jesus Christ — one may dance, another may bow, yet another may stand and shout. He is One Lord, but He has created many people.

We must never bring people to Christ and then insist to them, "Now, be just like me." We need massive diversity in programming, in our praise, in the expression of our spiritual gifts. In the church, we have divided ourselves in just about as many ways as we can be divided. We've divided ourselves by denomination . . .

means of baptism . . .

timetables related to the tribulation . . .

types of services . . .

and meanings for communion. It's time we recognize that the Lord meant what He said when He inspired Paul to write:

- "For we being many are one bread, and one body: for we are all partakers of that one bread" (1 Corinthians 10:17).
- "There is neither Jew nor Greek, there is neither bond nor free, there is neither male nor female: for ye are all one in Christ Jesus" (Galatians 3:28).
- "There is one body, and one Spirit, even as ye are called in one hope of your calling; one Lord, one faith, one baptism, one God and Father of all, who is above all, and through all, and in you all" (Ephesians 4:4-6).

Fads come and go in the church, just as they come and go in society. Prophecy is big right now — people are all looking for the "prophetic word." Some only want to go to services that are labeled "healing services." This one will lay hands on the sick, that one will call out diseases, another one might throw holy water on those with sickness.

The methods and fads don't matter. We serve One Lord. He is faithful to remain the same yesterday, today, and forever. He works through a multiplicity of ways and through all manner of gifts.

It is only when we feel truly free to be ourselves, however, that we allow other people to be truly free to be themselves. The person who enjoys the unique ways in which God has created him, is a person who is likely to appreciate and enjoy the unique way in which God has created others.

Our goal is to preach, teach, and experience truth — not culture.

There's more than one way to skin a cat.
There's more than one way to bake a cake.
There's more than one way to praise the Lord!

It's not just Satan who has bound God's people in their praise. *We* have bound each other in order to promote our own causes, agendas, and preferred styles.

You may not like the way another person expresses his faith in Christ. You may not agree with it fully or choose to adopt it as your means of expression. But you *must* value his right to express his faith in Christ the way he believes the Lord is leading him to express it. And don't waste your time criticizing him and become a prisoner in your own mind . . . heart . . . emotions!

There are many ways to praise the Lord. A person might dance, walk, stand with his arms raised, fall on his knees, lie flat on his face before God. He might sing, shout, talk, cry, laugh. What's important is that a man find a way to open up and express himself to the Lord. There's no "right" position or "right" form of expression for praise — the only thing that must be right before God is a man's heart, humbled to praise Him from the depths of his emotions.

When the world sees Christian men dropping their differences and coming together, the world is going to want what Christians have.

Politicians, educators, economists, scientists, and corporations — they have all tried unsuccessfully to bring the world together and to bridge the gaps that divide nation from nation, tribe from tribe, people from people.

But only God can build that bridge.

And the good news is that God does build that bridge by His outpoured Holy Spirit.

True Pentecost comes when devout men come together from every nation under the one anointing of the Holy Spirit. Regardless of their backgrounds . . .

> races . . .

>> cultures . . .

and denominations. You cannot have a genuine Pentecost outpouring of God's power in the presence of segregation, alienation, or separation among God's people.

When the world sees Christian men coming together under one anointing, it is going to run to our upper room to hear the Gospel.

Yes, indeed. When we are loosed in our hearts of all prejudice . . .

> loosed from our emotional bondage . . .

>> loosed in our praise and worship . . .

>>> and loosed in our ability to love others as God loves them . . .

the world will begin to turn to Christ for forgiveness, deliverance, and healing. It will *run* to the cross.

Loose that man inside you — and let him be free in Christ Jesus!

Getting Up From
Your Lame Position

Waiting on Man to Get Into Position

Things must be in place before God will act. The Bible tells us that at the beginning of creation, God had not caused it to rain upon the earth.

This does not mean that the earth was without water. Up to this time, God had caused a mist to come up from the earth to give moisture to the earth. There had been no downpour, however, from the heavenlies.

Why? Because there was not a man to till the ground.

There are some things that God has planned to do, has made provision for doing, and desires to do that He will not do until man is in place to receive what God intends to give.

The blessing is there . . . in God's safekeeping.

The need is there . . . insistent, resistant, persistent in its pain and suffering.

But the blessing won't be applied to the need until man's heart is in a

> These are the generations of the heavens and of the earth when they were created, in the day that the LORD God made the earth and the heavens, and every plant of the field before it was in the earth, and every herb of the field before it grew: for the LORD God had not caused it to rain upon the earth, and there was not a man to till the ground.
> *(Genesis 2:4,5)*

position for God to act according to His own laws of redemption, healing, and deliverance.

There are some things that God has in the heavenlies that will not be released to you until you are in the proper position spiritually, relationally, emotionally. Oh, you may be experiencing a "mist" — but in your spirit, you have a restlessness that there must be something more. You have an inner knowing that you aren't fully where you ought to be. You have an uneasiness, a frustration that causes you to say, "Why am I no further than this in my life?"

Rather than blaming your wife, your parents, your boss, or your race . . . you are wise to ask yourself, "Is God waiting on me to be in a different spiritual position before He pours out a blessing on my life?"

When you are in alignment with God and His purposes, He *will* open up the heavens and cause it to RAIN on you! You'll experience such an outpouring of God's blessings that you won't know how to contain them.

Ask God today WHERE He wants you to be spiritually so that you might receive the downpour of His heavenly blessings.

Recognizing the Lame at the Gate

The lame man who was brought to the Beautiful Gate was incapacitated, and because he was in that condition, he needed special care. While other men walked in and out of the temple area, this man was carried to the temple.

There was nothing wrong with this man in many areas of his body — he could see, hear, touch, and speak. He could move his arms and upper torso. In fact, there was only one thing wrong with this man — his ankles had no strength.

If there is something wrong in only one area of life, however, and that area of weakness is severe enough, a man's entire life can be affected. The "operation" of a man's life — the function, the activity — can be so impacted that it will feel to that man as if *everything* has gone wrong. That was the case with this man. Only one thing was wrong with him, but that one thing created a whole-life problem.

Now Peter and John went up together into the temple at the hour of prayer, being the ninth hour. And a certain man lame from his mother's womb was carried, whom they laid daily at the gate of the temple which is called Beautiful.

(Acts 3:1,2)

When a man is handicapped, he needs to be carried. He cannot support his own life, pull his own weight, or operate in his own strength. This has nothing to do with whether or not the man is a good man in his heart and motives. It has to do with his having a bad problem.

The lame man's problem had made him dependent upon other people. His problem interfered to a certain extent with their lives — he had to be carried by other men to a place where he could beg, and then carried home at the end of the day. He could not get to where he wanted to be on his own.

This man no doubt felt discouraged and low in self-value. When a man has to be carried about, unable to move about on his own, he feels demeaned. When a man has to beg for a living and is not allowed to participate fully in the activities of other men, he feels diminished.

Not only was this man lame in his ankles, he had a lameness in his emotions and his spirit. One area of weakness had created another in his life. Not only were his ankles lame; he was lame.

Virtually all men are in that position today. We each have a weakness in our lives that keeps us from functioning as a whole person. But what do most of us do? We deny our own lameness. And we pass by others who are lame because we don't have either the courage or the compassion that it takes to stop and help them.

It's time we quit kidding ourselves. We each have a need for God's healing power. Others have needs, and they need for us to help them experience God at work in their lives. Yes, we are all lame at the gate at some point in our lives, in some area of our lives.

The good news is that God sends people to the gate where we sit to help us receive what God has for us to receive. Watch for that person in your life. Look for that person to come. And be very aware that *you* may be the person that God is sending to bring deliverance to a lame man.

Be on the alert for a person who may be sitting at a gate through which you will pass today.

What Are
You Expecting?

What do you want when you go to church? Why are you really there? What is it you are seeking?

Are you present only so that you can tell others that you go to church? Are you there so that you can play a role that you think gives you some kind of status in your community? Are you there just to keep peace in your family and to avoid the nagging and pleading of your wife or your mother or your children?

Jesus once asked a group of people concerning John the Baptist, "Who did you go out into the wilderness to see? A reed shaken with the wind? A man clothed in soft raiment? A prophet?" (See Matthew 11:7-15.)

It's an important question for us to ask ourselves: Who are we going to church to see and hear?

If we are going to church just to hear the choir sing or to hear a preacher speak, we are making the same mistake

> And a certain man lame from his mother's womb was carried, whom they laid daily at the gate of the temple which is called Beautiful, to ask alms of them that entered into the temple; who seeing Peter and John about to go into the temple asked an alms.
>
> *(Acts 3:2,3)*

that the lame man made when he was carried to the Beautiful Gate that day. He was looking for the wrong thing. He was seeking alms. He wasn't expecting healing.

We also need to ask ourselves some serious questions about the way we regard the people we meet on a day-to-day basis: How are we looking at other people? What do we expect from our encounters with them?

So often we approach people the same way this lame man did. We are looking for what they are going to do for us. We are looking for what we can get from them. We aren't looking for what it is that God wants to do in us or through us.

I call this a "get-over" spirit. The person with a get-over spirit is always looking for someone or something to help him get over his problem. He's looking for what he can take from others, or what they will give to him freely — which is no different than alms-begging — without any effort or responsibility on his part.

People with a get-over spirit are users. They use people, but don't really love them. They latch onto people and seek to take from them what they desire or lust after — it may be sex, it may be money, it may be fawning adoration. They have little interest in other people apart from what they can get from them that will help them make it from today to tomorrow.

God calls us to see Him when we see other people. He calls us either to give to other people as He would give to them, or to receive from other people as if we are receiving from the Lord Himself.

When we go to church, we are to go with an expectation that *God* is going to speak to our hearts and heal our lameness.

When we encounter other people, we are to regard them with love and compassion — open to receive what good thing they may say to us to encourage us in the Lord, and also open to say and give to them whatever the Lord prompts us to say and give.

In this way we live in freedom — freely receiving and freely giving. (See Matthew 10:8.)

Identify precisely what you are expecting from God today.

Why Are You Who You Are?

Have you ever stopped to think about who you are and how you got to be who you are? Have you wondered how it is that you got through all the things you have been through? Have you ever thoroughly considered your own life?

So many men are so busy looking at their lame ankles — their problems, their needs, their area of weakness — that they fail to see the big picture of their own lives. They don't have an awareness of where they are in their lives, primarily because they don't have a clear picture of where they have been.

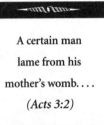

A certain man lame from his mother's womb....

(Acts 3:2)

This man who was carried to the Beautiful Gate had not become crippled as the result of an accident or an illness. He hadn't fallen from a rooftop or been thrown from a horse or been run over by a cart. He had been born lame. He had never known anything other than lameness all of his life. His lameness was not a disease, but a *weakness*. The bones of his feet and ankles simply had never gained strength.

This man actually had two advantages that many men do not have today.

First, the lame man knew that he had a problem. His lameness was obvious — not only visible to others, but visible to himself. He had to face his problem; there was no way to avoid it or ignore it.

Many men today haven't faced their lameness. They think that because they can look in the mirror and not see any major flaws, or get through a social event without making any major mistakes, or keep a job without getting fired . . . things must be all right. The fact is, we *each* have an area of lameness in our lives. It's there — even if we refuse to face it, even if it isn't obvious.

Second, the lame man knew the reason for his lameness. He knew the cause of his problem. He knew the "why" for his life being the way it was.

One of the things we each must do about the area of weakness we have in our lives is to trace it back to its origin. We need to ask, "*Why* am I like this? *Why* do I do what I do?"

Until we know why we are so angry . . .

so filled with hate . . .

so resentful and bitter,

we cannot understand fully what it is that we need to do to get beyond our problem.

Why do I come home from church where I've been acting like a saint and leaping about in praise like David . . . only to act like a wild gorilla with my wife and children?

Why don't I know how to communicate? Why am I unwilling to learn how to communicate better?

Why do I feel an inner rage all the time? Why do things often spin out of control?

Why am I not succeeding more at work?

Why do I feel depressed at times?

Why am I not growing more in my spiritual life?

Why am I not further along in my walk with the Lord?

Why am I who I am?

Get your own résumé and read it to yourself. Look back over your life. Face your life. Find out why you have been camping out in a state of lameness for so long.

Taking a look at your own life can be depressing if that's the point where you *end* your search of self. But if you use your new understanding to say, "This is how I got where I am, and here's what I am going to do about it," then your self-exploration can be highly positive.

When we look closely at our lives, we each discover that we need a Savior, we need a Lord, and we need relationships with other Christians who will teach us God's Word and build us up in Christ Jesus. That's one of the greatest discoveries a person can ever make.

There's a reason that you are who you are. But there's an even greater purpose for your life. You may be who you are, but you are not yet who you will be! God has bigger and better things ahead for you. We each are called to be a "partaker of the glory that shall be revealed" (1 Peter 5:1).

Consider today not only your problem and its cause, but your calling in Christ Jesus and its result!

Alive and Available

Where are you on God's agenda? Do you know?

The Bible doesn't tell us how long the lame man sat at the Beautiful Gate, but I feel certain that being carried to the gate was his daily habit. He had no reason to think that the day he encountered Peter and John was any different from any other day in his life. To him, it was probably "just another day" of begging alms.

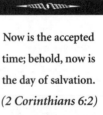

Now is the accepted time; behold, now is the day of salvation. *(2 Corinthians 6:2)*

Most of us don't know what day it is on "God's calendar." We don't know the day that is *the day* that God has marked on His timetable for us to receive our miracle. We very often aren't aware that God has a life-changing, mind-altering, spirit-redeeming, soul-cleansing miracle for us . . . today.

The challenge to us is to be aware of our miracle moment when it comes. And the only way I know to be aware of that moment is to stay aware always. We must be available *continually* to receive from God *continuously*.

Being ALIVE is the first requirement for being available. The good news is . . . *you ARE alive!*

In spite of the pain and weakness in an area of your life . . .

in spite of not being able to do what other men are doing . . .

in spite of not being able to move about like other men move about, walking and leaping about with full freedom of mobility . . .

the fact is,

you are still here! You have survived to this moment.

No matter how broken

or wounded

or frustrated you may be, you are alive!

And as long as you are alive, a miracle is possible. To receive a miracle of any kind, however, you must be *available* for a miracle.

Miracles happen to those who know they need them and make themselves available to receive them. So the devil would much rather see you so active and busy that you never give God or your life or your weakness a moment's thought. The devil would much rather see a man become completely involved with contracts and opportunities and business trips and too-full schedules than to see a man be brought to a place of being available should a servant of God walk by or should a servant of God come to speak a word from the Lord.

Being available means that we are . . .

- *alert.* We're looking for a miracle.
- *ready.* We have our hands lifted in praise, ready to receive.
- *excited.* We have a sharp, eager anticipation about what God is going to do.

Jesus said to His disciples — including us — "Your time is alway ready" (John 7:6). Let's live with that degree of availability!

Stay available today to receive the miracle that God has on its way.

Guarding Your Most Precious Spirit

Many people have security systems for their houses, or alarms for their cars. They know they have something of value. And they also know that there are thieves loose in the world who are likely to want the valuable possessions they have.

> The thief cometh not, but for to steal, and to kill, and to destroy: I am come that they might have life, and that they might have it more abundantly.
>
> *(John 10:10)*

While this is true for material possessions, so many men do not have a security system for their emotional and spiritual lives. Part of the reason is that they don't know *they* are valuable to God. And another part of the reason is that they don't know that a thief is loose in the world who wants to steal, destroy, and kill everything of value that they possess.

You can put bars on the windows of your house . . .

You can put an alarm system on your car that will cause sirens to sound and lights to flash on and off . . .

You can put video cameras and silent alarms in your store . . .

You can put padlocks on your bicycle or on trunks filled with things you hold to be valuable . . .

You can put your most prized possessions in sealed vaults with highly sophisticated security systems . . .

But are you putting something in and on and around yourself to guard your precious emotional and spiritual life from the ravages of the thief who wants to steal from you your very life?

You were created in the image and likeness of God. That's the only reason the thief needs to want to rob you of *who you are*. He knows that first and foremost you are an offspring of the omnipotent, omniscient, omnipresent, all-loving God.

You are a spirit . . .

that has a soul . . .

and lives in a body that was formed from the dust of the earth. Your spirit comes from God's "is-ness," and therefore you can know God in your spirit.

In your spirit you have God-consciousness. You have an awareness of Him and a desire for Him.

In your soul you have self-consciousness. In your mind, your psyche, your memories, and your emotions you know who you are and what you are supposed to do.

In your body you have world-consciousness. In your body, you know if you are hot or cold, hungry or satisfied, comfortable or uncomfortable.

The thief is after you solely because you have a part of God's eternal Spirit in you.

Guard your spirit. It's not only the most valuable part of you, it's the eternal part of you.

How do we guard our spirits?

First, build your relationship with Jesus. Spend time communicating with Him. Draw your identity from Him.

Second, build yourself up in God's Word. Read your Bible. Study it. Bind the Word of God to your mind.

Third, build up yourself spiritually in praise. Worship the Lord. Serve Him in every way you know.

Stay on guard. The thief never sleeps.

Look for the abundance that is found in Jesus. He has come to RESTORE whatever the thief may already have taken from you.

When You Know Who, You Can Find Out Why

When God blew from His own breath into the dust body of man, man came alive and knew who he was and Who God was.

Your understanding of yourself and your understanding of God are intricately intertwined. You cannot know fully who you are until you know Who God is. Until you recognize that God is the One Who has given you your life — the One Who has formed and fashioned you with a specific plan and destiny in mind — you cannot find either peace or a sense of purpose. It's time we stopped letting other people breathe on us their plans and start looking close into the face and heart of God for our identity.

> The spirit of God hath made me, and the breath of the Almighty hath given me life.
>
> *(Job 33:4)*

Until we allow God to breathe upon us and breathe into us His Spirit, we will be vulnerable to any person and anything that comes along that seeks to define us, and in defining us, manipulates and controls us.

There are many men who get up every day "just swinging," just beating the air. They are in a fight, but they don't know what they are fighting about. The person who is just flailing away is a man who is without purpose or goals, without direction or impact. He senses he is in a struggle but he doesn't know who with. The result is that at day's end, he is exhausted, frustrated, and angry. He has virtually no ability to win.

But the man who gets up every day knowing who he is battling is a man who can fight with purpose and intelligence and direction.

In order to win you must know that God is the Source of your life and that you have an enemy of your eternal spirit, and that God your Source will help you *defeat* your enemy. It is only when you come to that awareness that life makes sense.

If you don't know that God is your Source and the devil is your enemy, life can overwhelm you. There are too many issues and situations that just don't make sense, don't connect, don't produce as they should, or don't fit.

Say to yourself today, "The Spirit of God has made me. The breath of God is giving me life."

Don't let anyone breathe his or her identity or plans into you except God.

Pleasing to the Father

When Jesus stepped down into the Jordan River to be baptized by John the Baptist, He stepped into the fullness of God's purpose for His life. Jesus' step into the Jordan waters was symbolic of His perpetual death and resurrection.

Have you ever stopped to think that by the time Jesus stepped into the waters of the Jordan River that day, they were teeming with the sins of mankind? John the Baptist had baptized countless people in the Jordan, their sins figuratively passing from them into the sea of God's forgiveness, just as the waters of the Jordan River end up in the Dead Sea.

> This is my beloved Son, in whom I am well pleased.
> *(Matthew 3:17)*

From the shores of spiritual blindness, one might think, "How awful! Jesus was wading into sin." Jesus was doing so, however, to fulfill the purpose of God — redemption from sin. Jesus was *exactly* where God wanted Him to be, doing *precisely* what God wanted Him to do.

As Jesus stood in the very place God desired for Him to stand, God opened up the heavens, the Spirit of God descended upon Him, and a voice spoke from heaven saying, "This is My Son. This is My seed, My Son, Who pleases Me!"

Don't expect God to speak up for you — or to cause others to see you for who you really are — until you are willing to step into the place where God has called you to be. When you step into that place where you are supposed to be, you don't have to speak up for yourself, fight for yourself, or demand anything of others. God will speak for you. He'll command whatever forces are involved to yield to you, give to you, honor you, listen to you, obey you.

Don't expect God to open up the heavens and pour out His Spirit of power and truth and wisdom and righteousness onto your life unless you are where you are supposed to be. When you step into the place God has destined for you, you won't have to take on your own battles, grope about for the right decisions, or wonder if something is right or wrong. God will give you every ability you need. He'll put into your path what you need to have. And you won't have any doubt that it's God Who is providing for you or working in you.

To please the Father ... obey Him. Even if it means wading into someone else's muddy waters.

Go only where God calls you to go.
Once there, do only what He commands
you to do. You will be pleasing to Him!

The Enmity Between You and the Devil

Are you fully aware that the devil is after you? Do you have a keen sense that the devil is on your trail?

Yes, you.

You.

You.

YOU.

We sometimes think, "Oh, yes, the devil is alive and lurking about today, but he's not after *me*. I don't have anything he wants. I'm nobody. I'm not called by God to do anything spectacular. Why would the devil want me?"

He wants you because you are a potential seed for producing a harvest for God in this earth!

God prophesied to the serpent that had seduced Eve into sin that He was going to put enmity between the *seed* of the woman and the serpent. This word for seed, *zera* in Hebrew, is also a word used for semen. Women don't have

> And the LORD God said unto the serpent . . .
>
> I will put enmity between thee and the woman, and between thy seed and her seed; it shall bruise thy head, and thou shalt bruise his heel.
>
> *(Genesis 3:14,15)*

semen. The seed of the woman, therefore, was to be a "man-child" descendant of Eve.

This prophecy was fulfilled in Jesus Christ, but that fulfillment in and through Christ is ongoing in *us* until the day God brings this age to an end. The devil is a defeated foe in the context of eternity, but he has not yet been defeated fully in the context of earthly time. He still has access to men, women, boys, and girls to tempt them into sin. He still has an opportunity to lay a claim on the souls of mankind.

Therefore, there's enmity between you — one of the human seeds born down through the centuries from your great ancestor Eve — and the devil. Paul wrote to the Romans: "The God of peace shall bruise Satan under your feet shortly. The grace of our Lord Jesus Christ be with you" (Romans 16:20). The devil's hate is still raging against you.

Enmity is a state of ill will or hostility. It doesn't come and go. It remains the devil's intent to destroy you no matter what you do. His nature is the nature of a violent murderer who is on the lookout for his next victim. In 1 Peter 5:8 we read, "Be sober, be vigilant; because your adversary the devil, as a roaring lion, walketh about, seeking whom he may devour."

The devil is stalking you. He hates you. He is in a state of perpetual ill will, hostility, and conflict with you whether you know it or not. He is after your self-esteem, your identity, your mind, your emotions, your wife and children, your job or your business, your church, your well-being, your witness, your productivity, your health. He's after everything you value and hold as being good. Ultimately, his goal is the destruction of your eternal spirit.

Throughout the centuries, this warfare of the devil has been aimed primarily at the man-child. The devil's primary battles have been against men. When Pharaoh looked at the Hebrews and determined that they were becoming too numerous and too powerful, he didn't authorize the killing of all the Hebrew babies — no, only the male babies. (See Exodus 1:22.) Pharaoh didn't have an understanding that the Messiah would one day be a man born to an Israelite virgin. The one who knew this fact was the devil; Pharaoh was simply one of his pawns. And therefore, Pharaoh's order was that any time a man-child was born, the midwives were to kill him.

The devil is after you. He wants you. He seeks to kill you.

The devil doesn't mind your coming to church. He just doesn't want church — the Spirit of God — to come into you.

The devil doesn't mind your holding a position. He just doesn't want you to occupy *the* position you're supposed to hold in the kingdom of God.

The devil doesn't mind your having a title. He just doesn't want you to operate in your divine calling.

I have traveled the nation in recent years and have seen the power of God work in marvelous ways. Let me assure you, when men begin to move into the positions that they are called to occupy in the body of Christ, things happen! They happen both individually and in churches.

Are you in the position you are supposed to be in with God?

Being in the right place with God is the only way you can remain secure in the face of the devil's assault against you. To stay alive, stay connected to God as the Source of your life.

To stay alive in your spirit, stay alive in God's Spirit. That's the only way you will defeat the devil every day.

Don't Let the Devil Destroy You!

You don't have long on this earth. Even if you live to be a hundred years old, or older, you are going to look back on your life and think, "It's only been a few days that I've been alive."

In some communities and among some groups of people in our nation today, man's days are especially few indeed.

All around us we see man killing man.

Man gunning down his fellowman on the street . . .

> Man lying lifeless in crack houses . . .

> > Man curled up on street corners, homeless but too drunk to do anything about it . . .

> > > Man suffering in a hospital bed, HIV positive, until he breathes his final breath.

All around us we see men killing their seed, their *zera*.

Man that is born of a woman is of few days, and full of trouble.

He cometh forth like a flower, and is cut down: he fleeth also as a shadow, and continueth not.

(Job 14:1,2)

Men making babies and then not having the desire or taking the time to be fathers to them . . .
men impregnating women and then not marrying them or caring about their *zera*, encouraging women by their lack of involvement and provision to get abortions . . .

men abandoning their children and teenagers, leaving their sons to struggle with finding their own identity in a godless world.

If there ever was a mission field in need of a missionary, it's the mission field of the men in our nation. It's easier to get ten women to come to church, and then to love and serve God, than to get one man to do so.

What are we doing to God's seed? How are we destroying our lives? Wars and plagues don't need to cut down our men anymore. We are cutting down ourselves!

Who molested our boys and girls?

Who raped our women?

Who beat our toddlers?

Who abandoned our babies?

If the devil can't destroy your seed, he will do his best to damage your seed — to make it lame in some way, to make it weak in the ankles, to limit the effectiveness and strength of the seed.

We've all hurt some people . . .

    betrayed some covenants . . .

        made some mistakes . . .

            blown some money . . .

                missed some opportunities . . .

and sinned against God. But thank God, He is merciful.

The good news — the very BEST news — is that God forgives.

He forgives the molester . . .

He forgives the abuser . . .

He forgives the addict . . .

He forgives the liar and the thief . . .

He forgives the SINNER.

And He doesn't stop there. He heals the situation that sin created. He restores men to wholeness and changes their circumstances into a blessing.

The devil may be out to defeat you, but God is out to defeat the devil. Stay on God's side. Receive His forgiveness. Walk in His commandments. Praise His holy name. In staying on God's side, you are staying on the winning side.

Make every day you live a day that you CHOOSE God's life over the devil's death.

Are You Stuck at the Gate?

This lame man was laid daily at a gate that was so beautiful it had Beautiful as its name! If a man has an ugly problem, it matters very little that he is in a beautiful place. A person with an ugly problem has very little ability to enjoy beauty or appreciate it.

A certain man lame from his mother's womb was carried, whom they laid daily at the gate of the temple.

(Acts 3:2)

Not only that, but this man was living in the Promised Land. Yet he had very little ability to receive the fullness of the promises that others were receiving. As a lame man, he was not allowed into the temple. According to the law, his condition made him unworthy to participate in the rituals that able-bodied men kept.

So many men are close to being in the right place, but they aren't yet fully there.

They are just close enough to the church to know what's going on — to know who's who and what's being preached. But they are not all the way into the Body of Christ so they can experience the fullness of God's power and provision in their lives.

They are stuck at the gate.

Some of them even know when to kneel and when to raise their hands. They know the songs in the hymnal and precisely what time the service should start and end. They've heard more altar calls than they can count. They know all the protocol. They take all the ritual of the church in stride and from a distance . . . but they never get all the way into the place where they can receive God's blessing.

What keeps them stuck at the gate? Their attitude.

They have the same attitude that they have in the world, an attitude that says, "I'm like this because nobody will help me. I'm the way I am because nobody will help me 'get over' to the place of blessing."

They bring their unrenewed minds into the church. They expect the church to change them and do for them in the same way they expect their bosses, or the government, or the neighborhood social worker to change their world and do for them.

Now you don't have to be poor or financially destitute to have a get-over spirit. You can be rich and still blame your problems on somebody else who you believe is failing to do for you what you think they should be doing for you. You may be a very wealthy business owner and still have a get-over attitude, blaming your employees or your competitors for keeping you from the success you think you should have. You can be a church pastor and have a get-over attitude, blaming the members of your church for not appreciating you the way you think you should be appreciated.

The worst attitude in the world is a get-over attitude regarding God — that you are expecting somebody else to provide for you what God alone can provide for you, and then blaming that other person or group of people for failing you and causing you to fail.

Nobody can be your Source but God.

And nobody can put you into a right relationship with God but *you*.

If you are stuck at the gate today because of your own bad attitude, repent of that attitude! Go all the way into the place where you can receive God's blessings for YOURSELF . . . DIRECTLY from God. The way to that place is praise and worship.

Created for Wholeness

God created man in His own image — whole.

So often we get into a numbers game in the church. We get all wrapped up in determining if God is one or three — a single entity or a committee, a unity or a trinity. The Hebrews didn't have this conflict about God. Moses said, "Hear, O Israel: The LORD our God is one LORD" (Deuteronomy 6:4). The Lord is whole. And that is the only perspective that is necessary. The Lord isn't fragmented or divided. God is full and complete, lacking nothing whatsoever.

God has never faced a question He couldn't answer. He has never faced a need He couldn't supply.

He never had a desire He couldn't fulfill.

He is altogether self-sufficient and perfect.

> This is the book of the generations of Adam. In the day that God created man, in the likeness of God made he him; male and female created he them; and blessed them, and called their name Adam, in the day when they were created.
>
> *(Genesis 5:1,2)*

And God made man in His likeness and image — *whole*. Male and female created He *them*. He called *their* name Adam.

This first whole man had dominion over everything. He had a position granted to him by his Creator.

One of the great differences between men and women is rooted in this: Man had position with God before he had a relationship with another human being. Woman was birthed in relationship.

We see today that men are positional and women are relational. Men are concerned about power and status far more than women. Men love titles. Women are concerned about their relationships: their children, their spouses, their friends. When men get together they ask one another, "What do you do for a living?" In the course of the conversation, they expect to find out what position another man holds in his company. When women get together they ask, "Are you married? Do you have children?" In the course of their conversation, they pull out pictures of their family members and give details about every one of them.

Man's first job was naming. If he called a giraffe a giraffe, it was a giraffe! He had dominion over his world. But when man looked around, he didn't find a mate for himself. God said, "This situation isn't good. Man is too much like Me. He's too self-sufficient, too self-contained."

When God made Eve He didn't reach down into the earth again. He reached into man. He said to Adam, "I'm going to reach into you and pull out of you something that I've already placed in you." Man was created with woman inside him. And out of the inner emotional and spiritual womb of man, Eve was created.

Jesus approaches us in the same way today. He says to us, "I've placed My faith and My Spirit and My life in you. I'm going to pull out of you something that I've placed in you. I'm going to bring My desire for your wholeness to a reality that you can fully experience."

Jesus said time and again to those He healed and delivered: "Be thou made whole." He saw people as being whole entities — spirit, mind, emotions, psyche, body, relationships — all linked together so tightly that it was impossible to separate or fragment the elements of man.

Wholeness is God's plan for you. Jesus came to make you whole in His way, His timing, and for His glory. His wholeness for you includes *whole* relationships.

Ask God to make you whole today and to reconcile you to wholeness in your relationship with your wife, children, and brothers and sisters in Christ.

Walking in Whose Likeness?

After Adam and Eve had fallen into sin and were expelled from the Garden of Eden, we read that Adam fathered a child, and the boy was just like him. Adam's son was born "in his own likeness" (Genesis 5:3).

Adam had been created in the image of the wholeness of God. Seth was created in the image of his fallen father.

> Adam lived an hundred and thirty years, and begat a son in his own likeness, after his image; and called his name Seth.
> *(Genesis 5:3)*

And throughout the generations, we men have been born in the image of fallen men. We bear their sin nature. How many times have we heard it said about ourselves, "He's just like his daddy"? In some cases, we are too much like our daddies. History repeats itself over and over and over again.

Daddy was angry and frustrated . . . now look at my temper.

Daddy couldn't stay with Mama . . . now look at my string of divorces.

Daddy was an alcoholic . . . now look at my drug addiction.

Daddy had girlfriends . . . now I'm involved in a relationship I have to hide.

Daddy was a workaholic . . . and now I spend fourteen hours a day at work.

Daddy wasn't affectionate with his children . . . and now I don't know how to hug and kiss my children.

We have an interesting and clear example of the way in which sin tendencies are passed along from father to son in the stories of Abraham and Isaac.

And Abraham journeyed from thence toward the south country, and dwelled between Kadesh and Shur, and sojourned in Gerar. And Abraham said of Sarah his wife, She is my sister: and Abimelech king of Gerar sent, and took Sarah. (Genesis 20:1,2)

Sarah looked so fine as an old woman that Abraham knew that when he entered the south country of Gerar, King Abimelech was going to take one look at Sarah and want her as part of his harem. And Abraham was right. Abimelech did come and take Sarah to be his concubine.

Abraham told Sarah, "Tell him you are my sister." Abraham knew that if Abimelech thought Sarah was his sister, he would treat Abraham better. But if Abimelech thought Sarah was his wife, he would kill him so he might have sole right to Sarah. Abraham was willing to tell a half-truth and allow his own wife to be raped by a heathen king in order to save his own skin. And not only that, in the process he was jeopardizing his own future, since Sarah at that time had not yet given birth to Isaac, Abraham's *zera,* his destined seed.

Abraham passed on his tendency toward deceit to his son.

In Genesis 26 we read that Isaac, the son of Abraham and Sarah, faced a famine where Isaac lived, and he went south in search of food. He also went to Abimelech, king of the Philistines, and "Isaac dwelt in Gerar" (Genesis 26:6). History was repeating itself.

In Genesis 26:7 we read:

And the men of the place asked him of his wife; and he said, She is my sister: for he feared to say, She is my wife; lest, said he, the men of the place should kill me for Rebekah; because she was fair to look upon.

Isaac wasn't even alive when his father had made the same statement about Sarah. And yet there it was — the sin tendency of his father appearing in his life.

We see the pattern again and again in the Scriptures.

When you receive Jesus as your Savior, you become a son of God. Paul says, "Wherefore thou art no more a servant, but a son; and if a son, then an heir of God through Christ" (Galatians 4:7).

No longer do you need to walk in the likeness of your earthly daddy. Rather, you are called to walk in the likeness of your heavenly Father, your eternal Abba, Daddy God. Determine that you will be more and more like *Him*, day by day!

Choose today to WALK in the image of your ETERNAL Father.

The Importance of a Father's Blessing

And it came to pass after these things, that one told Joseph, Behold, thy father is sick: and he took with him his two sons, Manasseh and Ephraim. And one told Jacob, and said, Behold, thy son Joseph cometh unto thee: and Israel strengthened himself, and sat upon the bed.... Now the eyes of Israel were dim for age, so that he could not see. And he brought them near unto him; and he kissed them, and embraced them.... And Israel stretched out his right hand, and laid it upon Ephraim's head, who was the younger, and his left hand upon Manasseh's head. *(Genesis 48:1,2,10,14)*

The blessing was passed down from generation to generation among the Israelites when fathers placed their hands upon their sons and spoke God's words over them.

Jacob was on his deathbed when Joseph came to him with his two sons so that Jacob might bless them. In blessing them, Jacob prophesied their identity.

Father to son.

Father to son.

Father to son.

The people of Israel understood who they were largely because individual men learned who they were from their fathers and their grandfathers.

In the last few years as I have traveled this nation ministering in conferences of men, I have encountered literally thousands of men who do not know who they are. They never have had fathers who would lovingly lay their hands upon them and tell them who they were — either in their human family, or in the eyes of God.

A man who grows up without a father grows up not knowing his name, his identity. A boy who doesn't have a father figure after which to pattern his life will run the streets looking for father figures to give him a sense of identity and a name. He'll find one eventually — most likely a gang. He'll take on their name and become a Red or a Blue or a Cryp or a Blood. He'll take on the identity of his "older brothers" in the gang who actually operate in the role of a father to him, telling him who he is and what he is destined to be and do.

If that boy doesn't run into the arms of a gang, he's likely to run into the arms of the corner dope dealer or crime boss. He'll give him a name — Freakin' Freddy or Jumping Jim or Slick Sam.

Every man-child needs a name. He needs an identity.

He can't get that from his mother. Mothers are capable of giving great love and encouragement to their sons, but they cannot give them their identity. Only a father can do that.

Jacob refused to die until he could lay his hands on his sons and grandsons and tell them who they were and what they were destined to do.

We must follow his example today. It doesn't matter if our sons are five or fifty years old. We need to put our arms around them and tell them that they are loved by us. We need to tell them who they are in God. We need to quote Scripture over them and tell them —

- *You are a lion's whelp, and your hand shall be in the enemy's neck. (See Genesis 49:8,9.)*
- *You are more than a conqueror. You can do all things through Christ who strengthens you. (See Romans 8:37, Philippians 4:13.)*
- *You are a son of the Most High God. You have been purchased by the shed blood of Jesus Christ on the cross. You are a joint heir with Christ — a prince of the King of kings. There's greatness in your bones and in your bloodline. (See Galatians 4:6,7.)*

One Sunday in our church, I called all of the young boys who had no fathers to come forward so that I might lay hands on them and prophesy over them and tell them who they are in the Lord. I looked up and found that a thirty-year-old man had come forward and fallen at my feet. He said, "Pastor, I know I'm not a boy, but nobody ever told me who I am. Will you lay your hands on me and tell me who I am? I'm hurting because nobody has ever blessed me like that."

Call your sons and your grandsons to you today. Lay your hands upon them and tell them that you love them and that God loves them and has a purpose for their lives. Give them an identity.

If you are a grown man, find someone who can truly be a spiritual father to you. Ask him to bless you and tell you who you are in Christ Jesus.

Give a blessing to your children today.
Talk to them about their identity
in Christ Jesus. Encourage them
with your love and faith.

Relying on God to Reveal Your True Identity

You are not who the devil or sinful people say you are. You are who God says you are. And sometimes you have to go directly to God to get your real name and your real identity.

That was certainly the case in Jacob's life.

All of his growing-up years, Jacob had been called a supplanter, one who got what wasn't rightfully his. Jacob's very name means "trickster."

Schemer, where's your coat?
Schemer, come into the kitchen.
Schemer, put on your overshoes.
Schemer, take out the trash.

Can you imagine as a boy growing up only to hear every time somebody called your name what they believed to be the most negative aspect of your character?

Hey, con man!
Hey, fat boy!
Hey, worthless slob!
Hey, bastard child!
Hey, doper!
Hey, crook!
Hey, unwanted baby!
Hey, crippled man!

Jacob grew up believing what others said about him — that he was a schemer, a plotter, a manipulator, a con man. And Jacob lived true to what was said.

He believed the lie about him until he became the lie. He tricked his father into giving him the blessing and the inheritance that was rightfully his older brother's. He tricked his uncle Laban in his care of Laban's flocks, and he hoped to trick his brother Esau in the way that he returned home to face his family.

And then all alone in the dark of night, Jacob had an encounter with God. He wrestled with God until daybreak and finally cried out to God, "Bless me!"

The Lord asked him, "What is your name?" Jacob replied, "I am who people have said I am. I am Jacob, the trickster, the con man, the schemer."

And God said, "No, you are not. You are Israel. You are a prince, the child of God, and you have power with God."

You may have done what people say you did, but you are not what people say you are.

When you start praising God, He'll tell you who you are. When you get into God's Word and ask God to reveal to you your identity, He'll show you who you are. He'll show you that you are —

The head and not the tail. (See Deuteronomy 28:13.)

Above only, and not beneath. (See Deuteronomy 28:13.)

Chosen for this generation. (See 1 Peter 2:9.)

More than a conqueror. (See Romans 8:37.)

Part of a royal priesthood. (See 1 Peter 2:9.)

A peculiar treasure. (See Exodus 19:5.)

The citizen of a holy nation. (See Exodus 19:6.)

Look to God to reveal your true identity. He alone knows ALL about you.

Who is God saying that you are . . . right now?

The Right Name and the Right Action to Go With It

When Peter and John came to the temple at the hour of prayer, they fixed their eyes on the lame man by the Beautiful Gate and Peter said, "Look on us." Peter didn't want this man to be distracted. If a person gets distracted, he can miss what God has for him.

Peter wanted this man to pay close attention to what he was about to do. He wanted him to *really* hear him. I believe he got right down into the face of that man and locked his eyes on that man's eyes so that everything else in that lame man's awareness was shut out. That's the way we need to deal with people who are in pain.

If we are the ones who are suffering, that's the way we need to look at Jesus. We need to get so close to Him, and look so directly into His eyes, that we

> Peter said, Silver and gold have I none; but such as I have give I thee: In the name of Jesus Christ of Nazareth rise up and walk. And he took him by the right hand, and lifted him up.
>
> *(Acts 3:6,7)*

don't see anybody else, we aren't aware of anybody else, we don't hear anybody else. We only hear and see Jesus.

And then Peter spoke to him with a name.

Every one of us needs a name that is stronger than the devil's name. . .

a name that is stronger than your problem . . .

a name that is greater than your need . . .

a name that is more potent than your pain.

That name is the name of Jesus.

Paul wrote, "At the name of Jesus every knee should bow, of things in heaven, and things in earth, and things under the earth; and that every tongue should confess that Jesus Christ is Lord, to the glory of God the Father" (Philippians 2:10,11).

It is the name of Jesus that is higher than any other name. The writer of Hebrews says, He is "holy, harmless, undefiled . . . and made higher than the heavens" (Hebrews 7:26).

There is no other name that can make whole the part of you that is lame. Only the name of Jesus.

But then Peter went beyond words. He did what needed to be done. This lame man by the Beautiful Gate heard what Peter said, but the words themselves had no visible effect on his life. You may hear a sermon and in your mind say amen, and then find that nothing changes in your life. People in great need all around you may hear about the love and mercy of God, the blood of Jesus, and the power of the Holy Spirit, and yet not experience any of it for themselves.

Peter put the name of Jesus into action. He reached down and took this lame man by the right hand and lifted him up. And it was *as* Peter pulled this man to his feet that the lame man's feet and ankle bones received strength. (See Acts 3:7.) This man who had never walked, didn't need any help walking. No, he only needed help getting up on his feet. Instantly, he was standing, walking, and leaping about as he praised God.

There are people around you today who need for you to speak the right name into their lives — the name of Jesus — and they need for you to help them get to their feet spiritually and emotionally, and in some cases, physically and materially. It is your hand reached out in love and compassion, with genuine help that is not born of sympathy but which is born of faith, that will help them stand. You don't need to be their crutch. You don't need to spend the rest of your life helping them. But you do need to pull them to their feet so that God can heal and strengthen the lameness in their lives.

If you are the one who is being helped to your feet by a Christian brother, then rise up in faith on the inside even as you are helped to rise. Don't place your confidence in the person who is lifting you or praying for you. Put your trust in the name of Jesus. He is the One Who will heal you of your lameness, strengthen you in your weakness, and cause you to walk in boldness. He alone is the One Who can make you whole.

God is desiring to work in you and through you today.

Speak boldly and act boldly when He reveals to you the person you are to help.

No More
Hiding Out

Dysfunction Is No Excuse

I n Genesis, the book of beginnings, we find the first fight in the first family between the first two brothers. We find our first example of dysfunction.

You can hardly turn on a talk show today without hearing people give this justification for their abnormal and often sinful behavior: I came from a dysfunctional family. As if that's supposed to be a legitimate excuse!

Oh, the words sound good and they ring true. The *excuse*, however, is lame. The reason the words ring true to us is because we all have a degree of dysfunction in our lives. The reason for the lameness of the excuse is this: we are *all* from dysfunctional families. *Every* family has an element of dysfunction to it. We are all the descendants of Adam and Eve, our great ancestors who fell from a state of perfect function. So, if *any* person is able to rise above dysfunction, then *all* people are able to rise above dysfunction.

> And Cain talked with Abel his brother: and it came to pass, when they were in the field, that Cain rose up against Abel his brother, and slew him.
>
> *(Genesis 4:8)*

Adam and Eve became the parents in the first dysfunctional family. They gave birth to a dysfunctional son, Cain. Murder and mayhem broke out among the first two brothers.

That same murdering spirit exists in the world today. We seem perfectly oblivious to the fact that we are all brothers — that we all have the same blood flowing in our veins. We allow ourselves to fall into the same competitive, jealous, angry spirit that Cain first manifested.

People sometimes have a "get him first" killing spirit, while at the same time they give an appearance of being courteous and cooperative.

You must face the reality every day that some of your problems stem from the fact that there is *somebody* who doesn't like your success. International wars have resulted from the jealousy of one man over another man's success or possessions. Is it any wonder that the minor skirmishes we face in the daily battles of our personal lives come from the same root of jealousy?

Your attitude today is something that is totally under your control. You choose. You choose whether you will be prejudiced . . .

> angry . . .
>> hateful . . .
>>> bitter . . .

resentful. It is in your power to make a decision about what you will think and how you will act.

Don't blame your actions on your dysfunctional family. Base your actions on an attitude born of functional faith. "The grace of our Lord was exceeding abundant with faith and love" (1 Timothy 1:14).

Rather than have a "get him before he gets me" attitude, choose to have a "give to him first" attitude. Such an attitude will be far more beneficial to you . . . not only now, but for all eternity.

Refuse to blame your circumstances on the dysfunction of men. Instead, place your circumstances in the path of the function of the grace and love of Christ.

We Are All the Children of Oppression

Nearly every person who came to America from another nation came to this nation as a wounded person — someone who was oppressed in the land where he or she lived before coming to America. Every group of people has a horror story to tell as part of their personal cultural heritage. The oppression may have had some distinctive qualities, but oppression in general is a common denominator for every group of people who came to America.

> God anointed Jesus of Nazareth with the Holy Ghost and with power: who went about doing good, and healing all that were oppressed of the devil; for God was with him.
>
> *(Acts 10:38)*

Oppressed people readily become oppressors. We know that molested children are the most likely children to become molesters, abused children are the most likely to become abusers, and so forth. Every victim can easily become a victimizer. Those who have had no control in their past are the most likely to seek the most control in their future.

Oppression is nearly always by "family." When the Jews were sent to the concentration camps, they were sent as families. When the Indians were put on reservations, they were put there as families. Our problem is never ours alone. It is by "family."

As a result, an attitude of oppression is passed down family by family, tribe by tribe, people by people. Just about every "family" thinks it is more oppressed than all other families!

A man can be oppressed but not be able to identify his feelings as being oppression. He only knows that he feels trapped and he's angry about it.

Anytime a man thinks that he cannot change things and that he has no options, he becomes filled with rage and becomes abusive or violent . . . or he becomes despondent and depressed.

Some men who are filled with rage are talking encouragement but walking defeat. They try to convince themselves that things can be better, but they only give lip service to such change. In their hearts, they feel trapped.

The man who feels trapped has no tolerance for people who tell him things that he needs to do or points out to him things that he has left undone. He has no capacity for hearing that the trash needs to be taken out, the children need to be disciplined, or the room needs to be painted.

The fact is, however, if you don't like your circumstances or your situation, you can change it.

Whatever is oppressing you — people, habits, addictions, circumstances — whoever or whatever your slave master happens to be . . . you are mightier with Christ than the thing that is oppressing you!

Jesus came to heal "all that were oppressed of the devil" (Acts 10:38). And that, sir, includes *you*. He came to set you free, and he whom the Son sets free of oppression, is free indeed. (See John 8:36.)

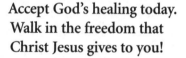

**Accept God's healing today.
Walk in the freedom that
Christ Jesus gives to you!**

You Have Been Favored by God

O ne of the things that Satan wants to keep you from knowing is that the favor of God is upon you and that you have been touched by Him and allowed to become the success that you are. Satan doesn't want you to give any of the credit to God. In fact, he doesn't want you to think that God has ever done anything for you at all.

Satan's lie is that a man has no purpose, power, or potential. The enemy does his utmost to get a man to buy the lie that he is broke . . .

> busted . . .
>> disgusted . . .
>>> oppressed . . .
>>>> depressed . . .
>>>>> and confused.

The enemy will try the race card, and if that doesn't work, he'll try the childhood memories card. And if that doesn't work, he'll dredge up all of your past sins and run them by

> By this I know that thou favourest me, because mine enemy doth not triumph over me. And as for me, thou upholdest me in mine integrity, and settest me before thy face for ever.
>
> *(Psalm 41:11,12)*

you. He'll remind a man of broken promises and broken dreams.

Satan works continually to build a case *against* God, never a case *for* God. The result is that some people have such low self-esteem that they don't believe God has touched them at all or that they have any possibility for success in their lives. Others are so arrogant that they think they've achieved all of their success on their own and that God hasn't had anything at all to do with it. Both groups of people are sorely wrong.

No matter how small your area of expertise or accomplishment may seem to you in your own eyes — that degree of success has been made possible because the Lord is on your side. You can't even hold up your own pants without the Lord giving you the strength and knowledge and ability to do so. You certainly can't raise a God-fearing family or contribute your talents to a job without God's assistance.

The irony is that often others are about to stab us to death — emotionally, spiritually, mentally, in our jobs, in our churches — and we don't even know why! We don't know that it's because others are perceiving the favor of the Lord on our lives and are jealous of it. We don't know that we have been blessed by God. We don't know that others are motivated to a great extent to act against us because they are jealous of what they see in us. How sad that they see what we don't see in ourselves!

Refuse to walk in ignorance of your own *God-given* blessings.

Praise God today for His FAVOR shown to you.

The Promised Land of Your Life Right Now

Y‌ou can be in the right general area for your success, but until you claim that area and move into it, you cannot possess the fullness of all that God has promised to you.

Are you in your promised land? Are you in your field of dreams?

If you answer no to those questions, it may very well be because you have a false concept of what it means to be in a place that bears the marks of God's favor and blessing.

> Be strong and of a good courage: for unto this people shalt thou divide for an inheritance the land, which I sware unto their fathers to give them.
> *(Joshua 1:6)*

Many of the old hymns in our churches talk about "Beulah Land," "Canaan Land," or "the promised land" — they all speak of a wonderful land "over there," one that we will experience in the "sweet by and by." Many of these songs came right out of a slavery mindset, but they have been sung for decades by both white and black people. Even today the idea is deeply engrained in us that we can only experience God's promises and blessings in the future, and very specifically in heaven.

That thinking is erroneous from a Bible standpoint.

When the Israelites went through the wilderness and arrived in the Promised Land, they encountered the Canaanites, the Jebusites, the Amorites, the Hittites, and a whole lot of other "ites" that didn't want them to settle in their area, much less take control over it. The Israelites had to do serious battle in order to *claim* the Promised Land that God had for them — the land to which God had called them, the land God had promised to them, and the land that God was going to help them conquer. The Promised Land wasn't a land they were going to enter after their death. It was a land they were expected to conquer during their life!

When you stepped through the blood of Jesus that flows from the cross, you stepped into your promised land.

Somebody else presently may be occupying the territory that God has for you — they may be in the job that God has destined for you; they may be living in the house that God has planned for you to own; they may be holding the office that God expects you to win in an upcoming election; they may be occupying the store or warehouse that God is going to help you purchase. Nevertheless, you are *in* your promised land. The Lord has led you to the place where He wants you to manifest His power and His greatness.

Keep in mind that you didn't arrive in the promised land of your life today by yourself. Neither did any Israelite man who crossed the Jordan River with Joshua to take claim to the land God had designated for them arrive there on his own. Each man came to that Promised Land with his family — either with his parents or with his wife and children. He came into the land with all of the other Israelites — his tribe and the other eleven tribes, as a whole, his people, his "church community."

The same is true for us today. You don't come into your promised land alone. Your acceptance of Christ involved other people and the claiming of your promised land still involves others. Factor in your family. Move as a whole family to the territory God is calling you to claim.

Take an inventory today of the things that God has promised to you. You'll find those things in the many promises that God has made to His people in the Scriptures. Every promise that is in the Bible is for you and your family *today*. Those promises are not for the hereafter. They are for NOW.

Target and then conquer a portion of your promised land today.

The Way We Come Into Blessings

Santa Claus isn't going to come and drop large bundles of God's blessings into your life. If you are sitting at the base of your fireplace with a glass of milk in one hand and a plate of cookies in the other just waiting for his arrival, you are going to be sorely disappointed.

Neither does God drop blessings out of nowhere. He doesn't sprinkle them around on the unsuspecting like so much fairy dust.

Receiving God's blessings into your life is a matter of warfare. This is not warfare waged with guns or knives or bombs. It is not warfare that is rooted in jealousy, anger, bitterness, or hatred. It is warfare against the true enemy of your soul — warfare in the spirit realm, warfare that is very real.

The kingdom of heaven suffereth violence, and the violent take it by force. *(Matthew 11:12)*

So many men are lacking in so many things today — things that must be won first in the spirit realm and then manifested in the natural realm — because they are lazy. I'm not talking about being lazy physically, or being lazy mentally, or being lazy on the job. I'm talking about being lazy spiritually. They don't want to have to *do* anything to bring about God's blessing in their lives. To get what you want you have to want it badly enough that you are willing to fight for it.

In the last several years, I've ministered to large groups of women and to large groups of men, and I've noticed a significant difference in the two groups. Women aren't at all reluctant to get into the trenches of spiritual warfare. I invite women to praise and worship the Lord, and then often I have to tell them when to quit so I can get on with my next point! They have no problem at all crying out to God or weeping unashamedly for the desires of their hearts — even if it means that their eye makeup goes streaming down their faces. They have no problem with raising their voices in prayer or laying hands on their sisters and rebuking the devil off their lives.

But when I invite a group of men to enter into the warfare of praise and worship, sometimes I'm lucky to get a couple of hallelujahs. If some men stand and praise the Lord for longer than thirty seconds, they think they've sacrificed a great deal of time and energy. Even under a strong anointing, some men find it difficult to enter into fierce spiritual battle.

Oh, they feel the anointing. You can't convince me that they don't feel what the Holy Spirit is doing. And they sense the power. You can't convince me that they aren't aware of the power of God or have a knowledge of what it is that God is desiring to do. The difficulty they have lies in their unwillingness to *express* what they feel and in their inability to *yield* their own pride to the power of God.

Unless a man is able to cross this hurdle and humble himself before God and engage in genuine praise and worship, he won't win the battles that are necessary for him to win in the spirit realm. He won't be able to lay claim to his promised land.

Be prepared to fight today in the spirit realm for the territory of blessing that you desire.

Giving to God What He Wants

Have you noticed that Superman is out? Clark Kent is the one everybody wants.

If you are offering Superman results to a woman today, you may attract her attention, but you won't be able to keep her affection. You may as well hang up your cape back in the closet.

> And the LORD had respect unto Abel and his offering: But unto Cain and to his offering he had not respect.
> *(Genesis 4:4,5)*

If you are choosing to be a stoic, strong superhero to your sons and daughters, you may impress them, but you will not fulfill them. Your children would rather be caressed by you than impressed by you.

The strong, silent type is out. Some of our fathers were so silent they never told our mothers that they loved them . . . they never told us they loved us. Some of them were so strong they never learned how to express themselves except through rage and abuse.

If you use accomplishments and power to replace affection and availability, you are not going to be regarded as a "king" by your wife and children. You are going to be considered as a heartless robot.

Machoism is dead. It's the sensitive and caring and vulnerable and available man who is desired today. If you are still offering machoism to the world, you are offering a product that nobody wants. Including God.

Your machoism placed against the standard of God's holiness and righteousness and compassion is about as impressive to God as a feather on the back of an elephant is impressive to the elephant.

God isn't remotely impressed by our approaching Him and asking, "What's up?" He isn't impressed by your résumé or your fancy suit. He isn't impressed by your expensive new wristwatch or your recitation of church history. He isn't impressed by your degrees or your pedigree. God is responsive only to those men who are willing to fall on their faces before Him, completely yielding everything to Him, and placing themselves in utter reliance upon Him.

An amazing thing happens when we learn how to bless the Lord — how to praise, worship, and exalt His name. We become more willing and able to bless our wives and children! In giving God what He wants, we are better able to give others what they truly need and desire from us.

God accepted Abel's offering because Abel gave God something that God wanted. Are you willing to give God what He wants from you today — a humble, open, loving heart filled with praise and worship?

Give God an ACCEPTABLE offering of praise today. He WILL receive and respect your sacrifice.

Moving the Heart of God

Until you learn how to move the heart of God, you will never be successful in spiritual warfare, and until you are successful in spiritual warfare, you cannot be completely successful in your life.

You may look like who's who and know what's what, but you will never possess all that God desires for you to have until you move the heart of God to "fight for you" and win the territory for you that He desires for you to have.

The first and foremost step for moving the heart of God is to break down the old man inside you and give him up. We dismantle the old man in us when we say with a genuine heart, "It's not about me, God. It's about You."

You can tell a lot about a man by listening to him pray.

I pray that You will endow us with all such endowments that may matriculate from Your throne, and cause us to enter

> And the LORD your God, he shall expel them [your enemies] from before you, and drive them from out of your sight; and ye shall possess their land, as the LORD your God hath promised unto you.
>
> *(Joshua 23:5)*

into various dimensions of glory. Even now as I stand on the crystal shore, I pray You will lead me into a place . . . .

Who are you trying to fool?

God doesn't need or want your egotistical, intellectualized image. In fact, He doesn't desire anything that is man-engineered or man-contrived. Including your flattery.

If a woman came to you and, measuring you up like a specimen in a lab, said to you, "You are a wonderful example of the male physique, with huge biceps and tight abs and a great smile," you might be impressed that she's impressed with your body. But her objective appraisal of your body is not going to be what would make you want to snatch her and hold onto her for the rest of your life. In your heart of hearts, you want a woman who knows the inner you and loves you anyway. And the same goes for God.

God desires for you to come to Him not with lofty words that express theological and historical facts about what He has done, but with a heart that is *dependent* upon Who He is and what He does and will do in order for you to take your next breath. He wants you to come with a desire to know Him, and with a willingness to lay your entire life bare before Him so He can heal you and restore you and create in you the likeness of His Son, Jesus Christ.

Cain tried to impress God — and Cain failed miserably. Cain gave to God something that he felt he had accomplished on his own. After all, he had tilled the earth and planted the seed and gathered the harvest. He came proudly to God, saying in his heart, "Look what I've done. Bless me on the basis of what I have accomplished."

Abel came to God and said in his heart, "I didn't do a thing. You caused this lamb to be birthed. You caused it to survive and grow. You provided the water for it to drink and the grass for it to eat. You are the Creator of all life. I'm giving back to You what *You've* done. I trust You with my life."

Ask yourself, "Is God receiving what I am giving to Him?" If you are giving Him a good front or a good line about yourself, He won't receive it. If you are giving Him your heartfelt praise and worship, He will receive your sacrifice of praise and bless you in return.

Look at yourself in the mirror today and say to yourself about your own egotistical pride, "Give it up." And then start praising God for Who He is and who He desires for you to become and who He is making you to be.

Where Art Thou . . . Really?

A re you in touch with where you are? How do you feel? Can you accept your own progress? Have you faced your faults, and also your great assets?

When God called to Adam in the Garden of Eden, He wasn't trying to find Adam. God knew where Adam was. Nobody and nothing can hide from God. No . . . God wanted for Adam to *admit* where he was. He wanted Adam to recognize fully who he was and what he had done.

> And the LORD God called unto Adam, and said unto him, Where art thou?
> *(Genesis 3:9)*

One of the most important questions you can ever ask yourself is this: Where am I in my life?

Men get into trouble when they don't know where they are.

So many men I've encountered are in one stage of their lives and acting as if they are in another. They have entered into marriage and fatherhood, and therefore, they have certain responsibilities, but they are still living as if they are boys playing in the park.

Even if you don't tell your wife . . .

Even if you don't tell your children . . .

Even if you don't tell your boss . . .

Even if you don't tell your pastor . . .

At least tell *yourself* where you are in your life!

When we hide, we turn phony. We act out a charade. We put on a "face" and participate in our own masquerade. Only two things are worse than being phony with other people: being phony with yourself and being phony with God.

If you haven't faced up to who you are and what you have done, you will find it very, *very* difficult to enter into praise and worship. Furthermore, you'll find it very difficult to relate to other men, or to their wives and children.

If you are feeling lonely and deprived, in all likelihood you are emotionally intimidated by other people. You can't open yourself up and give them a hug or pay them a compliment or look them in the eye with compassion because you are *afraid* they may look inside your heart and see the real you. Why are you afraid? Because you haven't looked there lately and you are afraid of what you might find if you do!

Until you face up to your flaws and failures — openly admit them to yourself and to God, and accept the fact that you aren't perfect — you'll never be able to allow other people to know, much less accept, your imperfections. If you aren't open to that kind of sharing, you will feel forever cut off, estranged, isolated, lonely, deprived, and alienated from other people.

Many men spend a lot of time and energy asking about the other men around them, "Where are they?"

What does that man have that I don't have to get that kind of woman?

What does that man do to be able to afford that kind of car and live in that kind of house?

How is it that HE has that kind of job and authority and power?

These are all variations of asking, Where is *he* at? The answer to that question leads to a dead end. It results in jealousy and competition and hatred and distrust and suspicion . . . all of which result in a murderous attitude.

Instead, ask *yourself*, "Where am *I* at?" That's the question that can lead to life. That's the question that will lead you to repentance before God, to an ability to get close to other people, and to fulfillment and true satisfaction in life.

Face yourself today. Answer God's question: Where ARE you?

Your Answer to God's Question

God called to Adam and asked him, "Where art thou?" And here's how the first man answered the first question that God had asked him: "I heard . . . I was afraid . . . I was naked . . . I hid."

Most men don't like open confrontation. I have known some physically big, powerful men who were afraid to go home to their five-foot-two-inch wives because they knew they would be facing a confrontation with her the minute they walked in the door.

> And he said, I heard thy voice in the garden, and I was afraid, because I was naked; and I hid myself.
>
> *(Genesis 3:10)*

In my years of counseling men who had a long history of being physically and emotionally and sexually abusive, I discovered that abusers are among the most fearful men I've ever met. They come across to their victims as being totally unafraid, but the fact is, they are *very* afraid of themselves and of being confronted with who they are. They rarely face themselves — they don't know who they are or where they are at — and they are highly fearful that somebody else might discover the darkness that they secretly know is inside them.

Men tend to talk very easily about things that don't really matter. But most of us men clam up when the talk turns to the things that matter the most. We hide.

You can't have a relationship with someone if you are hiding from a person.

Not a relationship with God.

Not a relationship with your wife.

Not a relationship with your child.

Not a relationship with the brother who stands next to you in the pew at church. Relationships are built when we stop hiding and face ourselves, and then allow ourselves to be vulnerable and open with other people.

A man sometimes acts as if he can't hear, or hasn't heard. The fact is, he heard — he just didn't like what he heard.

He heard his wife when she said she needed more time, attention, or consideration.

He heard his child when he complained that Dad wasn't around very much. He heard his daughter when she said, "I love you, Daddy," and he heard her sigh when Daddy didn't say anything back.

He ran and hid emotionally because he didn't know how to give to other people what they said they needed.

A man who is afraid and doesn't know what to do is a man who feels exposed. He feels undone. He'll go to great lengths to hide himself — to bury himself in his work, to get involved in an affair that doesn't require any vulnerability on his part, to put up a brick-wall facade around his heart to hide his true emotions.

So men end up afraid, frustrated, whimpering inside, locked up, impotent. And all the while, they are doing everything they can to cover up their inner feelings and emotional inadequacies.

Truth requires that you open up and share who you really are. It requires an honest answer to God's question, "Where art thou?" rather than an excuse rooted in your own fear.

Ask the Lord today to give you the courage to know yourself and then to reveal yourself to others.

Acknowledge Your Emotional Needs

What is the harm in keeping your fears and your emotional needs to yourself?

Because what you use to hide your fears and needs from others will eventually become a prison to you.

It will lock you up,

freeze you up,

bottle you up . . . and keep you from moving in to claim all that God has for you in your life.

Some men turn to alcohol or drugs in an effort to hide themselves from their fears and emotional needs.

Some turn to prostitutes — they won't trust their wives with their emotions, but they'll trust a total stranger with their bodies, their potential *zera* (seed), and their reputations.

Some turn to overwork — putting all of their energy into the job and burning the midnight oil — in an effort to avoid the need to relate to people.

Eventually, each of these escapes — and any other escape — becomes a prison. It traps you even further into a cycle of silence, because once you are entrapped by your escape mechanism, you won't want to tell anybody about that trap either. Your fear only grows greater as your silence grows deeper.

The fact is, God created you with emotions. He created you with a need to feel, to touch, to express, to have an emotional outlet and release. Look at a little boy. He's free to express himself, to vent his feelings, to hug and kiss and be hugged and kissed in return. He hasn't learned to hide yet.

What happened to you on your way to becoming a man?

Where art thou?

What caused you to feel that you need to run and hide?

There's another you behind the facade.

You need to be touched just as much as the next guy.

You need to be held.

You need to hear loving words, spoken in a gentle way.

Don't deny your emotional needs.

David wasn't afraid to admit to himself and to God that he was weak, afraid, sorrowful, angry, or in need of love. He even said that his heart melted like wax! (See Psalm 22:14.) In fact, the entire twenty-second psalm is *filled* with emotions. Read it!

The Bible says about Jesus that He was a man "who in the days of his flesh . . . offered up prayers and supplications with strong crying and tears"

(Hebrews 5:7). Jesus was a Man Who knew how to express His emotions.

Tell God you need Him.

Tell Him you love Him.

Tell Him you are in trouble in your life.

Tell Him where you ARE.

**Express your emotions to God today.
He created you to pray with FEELINGS.**

Breaking the Silence of the Lambs

God knew that Adam not only needed to know where he was at, but that he needed to say so.

Are you a man who turns off the lights at night, only to lie in the darkness of your own bed, unable to say to your wife, "I love you"?

Are you a man who, when your son comes to you, you respond with "Hey, what's happening, man?" instead of putting your arm around your son and giving him the hug that he really desires?

Many of God's men — God's sheep, His beloved lambs — are silent today.

They know who they are and what they have done, but they have lockjaw when it comes to talking about it, even in private confession to God.

They *know* they need to be held, but they'll never *admit* that they need to be held. Instead, they'll come home and say to their wives and children . . .

Why haven't you cleaned the house?

Why aren't you making better grades in school?

> Hear my cry, O God; attend unto my prayer. From the end of the earth will I cry unto thee, when my heart is overwhelmed: lead me to the rock that is higher than I. For thou hast been a shelter for me, and a strong tower from the enemy.
>
> *(Psalm 61:1-3)*

Why didn't you catch that fly ball that came your way?

They are scared that they are about to lose their job but they'll never say a word about it. Instead, they'll march around with a chip on their shoulders, as if to say . . .

What are you doing in my way?

Who gave you the right to tell me what to do?

Why are you showing favoritism to everybody but me?

They are afraid that if they tell what they feel, others will lose respect for them or will take advantage of them.

Our fears can erupt in anger and in criticism. But most of the time, they lie just under the surface of our stone-cold silence. As long as they remain there, they will ferment and brew . . . unhealed, unchanged, unresolved. We will remain weak on the inside even though we may seem strong on the outside.

David said, "O LORD my God, I cried unto thee, and thou hast healed me" (Psalm 30:2). Hasn't the time come for you to break your silence so God can heal *you*?

Make today the day that you break
the "silence of the lamb" in your life.
Tell God what you are feeling.
Tell your wife and children today how you
feel about them. Express to them what you
need emotionally — first, that you have
emotional needs, and second, what they are.
Open yourself up to receiving from
them the love they will give you.

Laying Your Head on Jesus' Breast

During the Last Supper, as Jesus was eating His final meal with His disciples before going to the cross, we read that John was "leaning on Jesus' bosom . . . lying on Jesus' breast" (John 13:23,25). Can you imagine what people would say about a man who did that today? Even if we knew the person was very spiritual, we'd probably raise an eyebrow.

But John had no problem with it. He knew that he was loved by Jesus. In fact, throughout the gospel of John, we find John referring to himself as the disciple "whom Jesus loved." (See John 13:23.)

John was open in his devotion to Jesus. Of all the disciples, only John is mentioned by name as being at the crucifixion. He is the only disciple to whom Jesus spoke directly from the cross. Jesus gave John the responsibility for Jesus' own mother. Jesus no doubt knew that, of all the disciples, John was the one most capable of expressing love to His mother.

> Herein is love, not that we loved God, but that he loved us, and sent his Son to be the propitiation for our sins. Beloved, if God so loved us, we ought also to love one another.
>
> *(1 John 4:10,11)*

I once did a study of the life of John and I discovered that John was the youngest disciple. Peter, James, and the others were probably in their forties at the time of Jesus' ministry, but John was very likely in his early twenties. John hadn't been corrupted yet into denying his emotions. He wasn't hiding. He wasn't afraid.

Love and showing love one to another is the hallmark of John's letters. (See 1 John, 2 John, 3 John.) It is the theme of John's gospel — "For God so loved the world, that he gave his only begotten Son" (John 3:16).

Are you aware that John is the only disciple that we know with certainty died of old age? All of the other disciples, about whose deaths we know, died in martyrdom. But John died peacefully at more than a hundred years of age. I personally believe that was because John had learned how to love people and how to express his faith with loving words backed up by loving actions.

If you want to live a long life and die in peace, I suggest that you lay your machoism down and lay your head on Jesus' breast.

Voice your love to God today. Then swallow your pride and fear and say to your wife, your children, and your friends, "I love you."

The Domino Effect of Your Praise

There's a domino effect that starts to manifest itself when you praise and worship God.

When you open up yourself to tell God how wonderful He is and how much you love Him and enjoy spending time with Him . . . you are very likely to find that your wife starts telling you how wonderful *you* are and how much she loves you and enjoys being with you.

When your wife starts talking to you like that, your children are going to overhear her at some point . . . and very likely they are going to start telling you what a great dad you are and how much they love you and enjoy spending time with you.

What happens to you in the process?

Your loneliness — that ache in your inner man that feels alone and isolated and hurting — is going to be healed. You're going to feel more courage and strength than you've felt before.

As you continue to go to God in open, free-to-be-yourself vulnerability and continue to praise and worship Him with your entire being, your love for Him is going to grow . . .

your love from and for your wife is going to grow, your love from and for your children is going to grow, and

your love for *yourself* is going to grow so that you can appreciate the good things that God is doing for you and in you and through you.

But as long as you starve God of the praises due Him, you are going to be starving yourself of the praises that you need. You'll find yourself living in an emotional wasteland, without love and deep appreciation from the very people with whom you *should* have the most loving relationships.

David said, "O magnify the LORD with me, and let us exalt his name together" (Psalm 34:3). The end result of your magnifying and praising the Lord is that your entire family is going to want to join you in magnifying and praising Him, and as they do, they will magnify and praise one another so that your home will become a haven of peace, rest, and emotional strength.

It's time we start saying to the Lord —
You are wonderful. There's nothing You can't fix.
There's nothing You can't do. There's no problem
You can't solve. There's no need You can't meet.
There's no issue too great for You. I'm casting all of

my care upon You. I'm giving it all to You. I'm giving
all of ME to You. I'm laying my head upon Your
breast, Lord. I know You love me and I'm relying
upon You to provide for me everything I need!
I'm not going to have this depression. I'm not going
to stress out. I'm not going to have this nervous
breakdown. I'm going to trust You to defeat my
enemies for Your glory. I'm trusting You to break
down the doors that are locked and to wax great on
my behalf. I'm relying upon You to win the victory!

When we praise the Lord, He opens up the gates of
His kingdom and sends forth His warriors to fight
and win the spiritual battle you are facing. They ride
on the wings of our praise.

It's time to break the silence!

**Give voice to your feelings,
to your needs, and to your praise.
Lay your head on Jesus' breast today!**

Refuse to Play the Blame Game

God asked Adam, "Who told you that you were naked? Have you eaten of the tree whereof I commanded you not to eat?" (See Genesis 3:11.)

Adam didn't answer either question. Oh, that he would have! Oh, that he could have been honest enough with himself to cry to God, "I have sinned. Have mercy on me!"

Instead, Adam tried to justify what he had done by blaming someone else. He said to God, "It's the fault of the woman you gave to be with me. She gave me of the tree, and I ate of it." (See Genesis 3:12.)

> And the man said, The woman whom thou gavest to be with me, she gave me of the tree, and I did eat.
>
> *(Genesis 3:12)*

How many men try that same line today?

I'd be a better husband, Lord, if my wife would just . . .

I could be a good father, Lord, but my wife . . .

I'd be further along in my life and in my career, Lord, if only my wife would . . .

I wouldn't get so angry and lash out with so much hatred, Lord, if my wife . . .

And if it isn't his wife who gets the blame, he might try to lay it on someone else.

I'd be more honest in my business dealings if my partner . . .

I'd have better control of my temper if my boss would just . . .

I wouldn't be like this if my parents . . .

I wouldn't have all these troubles if the people in the government . . .

The "blame line" didn't work for Adam, and it won't work for you. The situation in your life is not the *fault* of someone else. It's *your* responsibility.

Deal with yourself. And you'll probably find that those you have been blaming are not nearly the problem they were!

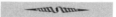

Come before God today and with an honest heart admit, "God, the problem is with me. Fix ME, Lord. Show me what it is that I must do in order to be forgiven and healed by You and to be free to forgive others and to heal my relationships with my wife, my children, my friends, and my coworkers."

Your Wrestling
Match With God

The Enemy
In-a-Me

In any group of men, I know in my heart that every kind of problem is present . . .
> every kind of need . . .
>> every kind of weakness . . .
>> every kind of struggle.

I also know that *today* is the time when we need to confront those problems, needs, weaknesses, and struggles.

It's time that we begin to challenge and confront ourselves about what we hold within ourselves.

I am not too concerned about the witches or witchcraft, or about demons, demonology, sorcery, or astrology. As bad as crime is, I'm not too concerned about the mugger, the rapist, or the con artist. What I am concerned about, however, every day of my life is *the enemy in-a-me*. If there's anyone you need to confront continually, it's yourself.

When a man ignores the commandments of God and refuses to turn to God and acknowledge Him as Lord,

And even as they did not like to retain God in their knowledge, God gave them over to a reprobate mind . . . being filled with all unrighteousness, fornication, wickedness, covetousness, maliciousness; full of envy, murder, debate, deceit, malignity.

(Romans 1:28,29)

the worst punishment God gives to that man on this earth is to turn him over to himself — to give him over to his own reprobate mind.

A popular advertising slogan in recent years had as part of its slogan — "have it your way." The problem is that when we seek to have it our own way, we literally self-destruct.

I am always amazed at how a man can look at another man and arrogantly say, "I'm better than that person." I'm not talking about racial or social distinctions here — I'm talking about the distinctions that we make about another person's sinfulness. When we make a claim that we aren't as sinful as the next person, we are, in effect, claiming that one type of sin — and in particular, *our* type of sin — isn't as bad as another type of sin. The man that draws such a conclusion doesn't know his Bible. The Bible says, "All have sinned, and come short of the glory of God" (Romans 3:23).

The fact is, the capacity for *every* type of sin resides in each one of us. We may not have done it, but chances are, we've thought about it! We each know that there are lots of things in our imaginations that we don't talk about. And if we haven't thought about it *yet*, given the right situation and circumstance, we *will* think about it and possibly even do it.

If you were pressed . . . or under certain stresses . . . or faced with certain alternatives, you'd have no problem at all in committing every sin in the book.

If a murderer entered your house and was heading for your child's room, would you have any second thoughts about stopping that man no matter what it took to do so?

If you and your family were starving and you came across a cart filled with food, would you have any hesitation about becoming a thief?

If you were told that you had to have sex with a certain person in order for your baby's life to be spared, would you say no?

In our human nature, we are totally depraved. We have an equal capacity to sin. And we each must face that capacity within us. We must confront our sin nature.

Thank God today that He has not turned you over to your own self, but that in His great mercy, He is still present in your life.

Your Life
Has Been Preserved

God isn't finished with you yet. You haven't arrived. There's still more to be done by you, and therefore, still more that needs to be done in you. God still needs to work on each one of us.

That truth doesn't scare me in the least. I'm just grateful that He's kept me alive long enough so that He *can* work in me! I'm grateful that He's poured into me what He's already poured into me, and I'm looking for anything else that He wants to pour into me because what He pours is always good!

> And Jacob called the name of the place Peniel: for I have seen God face to face, and my life is preserved.
>
> *(Genesis 32:30)*

We each know, if we're honest with ourselves, that the Lord has protected us or we wouldn't be at the point we're at today. We have to admit that His hand was on us long before we were saved.

When you were driving around drunk, an accident just waiting to happen . . .

When you were slapping your wife around and she was on the verge of calling the police . . .

When you were lying to that girlfriend to get her to do what you wanted her to do . . .

God was there. Even then. He had you in His grasp.

If God hadn't been merciful to us when we were sinners, we'd all be dead!

So often I see men who have been through so much in their lives that I am amazed they are still alive.

Anybody else would have self-destructed.

Some of their school classmates died.

Some of their teenage friends were murdered.

Some of their adult friends overdosed on drugs.

Through all of their troubles, they are still alive!

The devil has tried to take me out on numerous occasions, through one means or another, but I'm still here. And before I'll let him take me out completely, I'll tie a rag around my head and put a knife in my teeth and wait for him in the bushes! I'm prepared to do battle with the devil.

Some people get depressed too easily.

They become discouraged too easily.

They become suicidal too easily.

You've got to have a little Rambo in you!

I'm not giving up. I'm going to FIGHT. I'm going to HOLD ON. That's what Paul wrote to Timothy when he said, "Fight the good fight of faith, lay hold on eternal life, whereunto thou art also called" (1 Timothy 6:12). I refuse to give in!

Thank God today that He is still at work
in you. Refuse to give in to the devil.
Fight him every step of the way.

Refuse to Remain a Well-Marked Target

If you don't confront your own frailties and your own capacity for sin, you remain a well-marked target for the devil. If you don't admit that you are vulnerable to committing sin in a certain area, you remain vulnerable in that area. Why? Because in being so sure that you'd never commit the sin in question, you take no safeguards against it. And without safeguards, you are wide open to the devil's attack.

> He was manifested to take away our sins.
>
> *(1 John 3:5)*

You never thought you could get that angry.

You never thought you could be that hostile.

You never thought you could have an affair.

You never thought you could be that weak.

You never thought you could cheat in your finances.

You never thought you could leave your family.

And because you never thought you could . . . you did.

Look at yourself in the mirror and admit, I *could* commit every sin. I'm capable of it in my human flesh.

People may be saying to you, "You're going to have to deal with your problem." They see your problem as being drugs, or alcohol, or an affair. They may see your problem as being your temper, your hatred, your prejudice, your bitterness.

But I'm telling you, "There's a problem *behind* your problem" And that REAL problem is sin.

What is it that makes a thirty-five-year-old married man try to act like he's seventeen and single?

What makes a man want to drown his troubles in alcohol or use drugs to give himself a high?

Why does a man feel a need to prove himself by doing daredevil stunts?

The bottom-line answer is this: man's sin nature.

Your sin nature is your tendency to want to do what the devil tells you to do, more than you want to do what God tells you to do. It is your sin nature that is changed when you believe in Jesus Christ and accept Him as Savior, and then follow Him as Lord. John wrote, "He that committeth sin is of the devil; for the devil sinneth from the beginning. For this purpose the Son of God was manifested, that he might destroy the works of the devil" (1 John 3:8).

If you have never asked God to forgive you of your sins and change your sin nature, do so right now! God stands ready to forgive you. As 1 John 1:9 promises, "If we confess our sins, he is faithful and just to forgive us our sins, and to cleanse us from all unrighteousness."

Face your own sin capacity and then accept God's capacity to forgive you and transform you.

God Has Reserved a Place for You

Are you aware that God has made a statement about you in eternity?

God exists in eternity. We exist in time. When God says something, He says it in the context of eternity. That means that it *will* happen and it *will* last forever.

What has God said about you? God has taken a chair and placed it in the midst of His angels in eternity. Then, pointing directly at you, He has said to them, "This chair belongs to that man. I'm going to bring him right here for an encounter with Me. I'm going to do My best to love him until he receives My love and My forgiveness. I am going to make him into one of the jewels in My crown."

And when God speaks, He doesn't listen to any of the arguments that oppose His will.

But that man is a liar.

God says, "A liar is a bad thing to be, but it doesn't stop Me from loving him. I'm going to bring him into My presence. This chair has his name on it."

But he's a thief.

> God, who quickeneth the dead ... calleth those things which be not as though they were.
>
> *(Romans 4:17)*

God says, "That's not good, but it doesn't stop Me from reaching out to him. I'm going to bring him into My presence. I love him and I want him here."

But he's a molester.

God says, "That's a very hurtful thing to be, but nevertheless, I'm going to bring him into My presence so I can tell him I love him and desire to forgive him."

Murderer . . . homosexual . . . rapist . . . drug dealer.

God says, "I've got a chair with his name on it in My presence. I've got a plan for bringing him here to Me so I can love him and forgive him and live with him forever."

But he's a man who is violent emotionally and physically to everybody he meets.

"Yes," says God, "but when *I'm* finished with him, he's not going to be that way. In fact, he's going to be a deacon in his local church and he's going to be sharing the Gospel with men who are violent emotionally and physically."

I know men today who, ten years ago, would never dreamed of attending one of my conferences, much less praising and dancing and shouting before the Lord.

God calls those things which were not as though they were, because He knows He has the power to make them become what He says they will be. God does not have any doubts about His own ability to save, redeem, deliver, or transform a human life.

Furthermore, the seat that God is holding for you is *your* seat and nobody is going to sit in it but you. You don't have to worry about someone else getting your gifts or taking your place or earning your rewards.

Your enemies never thought you'd be there.

Some of your friends never thought you'd be there.

There were moments that even *you* thought you'd never be there. But the time came when you sat down in God's presence and He sat down with you, and you had an encounter with God and it changed your life.

His right hand and holy arm pulled you out of the place you were and placed you where you are. He has done, is doing . . . and *will do* . . . *ALL* that He has planned and purposed for you.

That's why God can call a person holy, blameless, and righteous while they are still confused, in trouble, in turmoil, and tied up. He knows His plan and His power. He knows that He *will* accomplish His purposes.

Thank God today for holding a seat for
you — for making you an advanced
reservation in His kingdom. Trust Him
to do in you all that He has planned.

God Wrestles With You . . . Alone

God maneuvers each one of us into a place where He can deal with us directly. He calls us to a state of "aloneness." He doesn't deal with us in the context of other people. Cliques, clubs, groups, and all sorts of entanglements, societies, and mentalities can keep us from hearing God as much as they can help us to hear from God. When God gets you to the point of dealing with the deep issues of your life, He does so one-on-one. Just you and God. Just me and God. Just each one of us alone with God.

> And Jacob was left alone.
>
> *(Genesis 32:24)*

Who are you really?
When nobody's looking . . .
    when you aren't "prepared" . . .
        when all the camouflage has been removed . . .
            when you don't have an ego to defend or anything to prove . . .
                when you aren't bogged down in imitations or concerned about status?
Who are you?

Anytime you are surrounded by people who don't know the real you . . .

Anytime you are in a situation where you can't fully be yourself . . .

Anytime you have to camouflage who you really are to be accepted . . .

You are alone. You will feel isolated, as if you are watching people through a glass wall.

When God is ready to do His divine surgery on you, He brings you to an "alone" place. Nobody invites guests into an operating room. Neither does God. His work on you is private.

When God begins to move in on your life and starts setting up His one-on-one appointment with you, you may feel very uncomfortable. In fact, I believe the first response of nearly all of us at that time is to try to surround ourselves with more and more people. We feel restless, frustrated, lonely in our spirits. We feel a greater need to have somebody with us, to protect us, shield us, wrap their arms around us, join us, walk with us. We soon discover that the presence of other people doesn't meet the need. The loneliness and restlessness we are feeling in our spirits is God's call to us. He is reeling us in to our one-on-one encounter with Him.

You can be surrounded by people . . . and still be alone.

You can have intimate relations with your wife . . . and still be alone.

You can have dozens of close friends . . . and still be alone.

It's when we admit that we are lonely and need something that people can't supply — we need Someone to fulfill a part of us that nobody else seems to be able to fulfill — that's when God steps in.

When you say that you are left alone, it means that somebody that you thought you could count on for protection has disappeared. You feel isolated, separated, apart. Alone.

When we feel left alone, therefore, our hope is usually that someone will come along and comfort us. In fact, we expect from our human standpoint that "comfort" is what a loving God would do to a man who is left alone. God says, however, that He is not coming to comfort, but to *confront*.

God came to challenge Jacob, to wrestle with him.

Jacob's first reaction was, no doubt, "Oh, no, not You too!"

Everybody is wrestling with me.
My wife is wrestling with me.
My children are wrestling with me.
My boss is wrestling with me.
My creditors are wrestling with me.
My coworkers are wrestling with me.
My church is wrestling with me.
My own mind is a wrestling match.

And now, You, too, God?

The Bible says, "Faithful are the wounds of a friend" (Proverbs 27:6). A true friend is one who "wounds" you for a good reason. What he says may hurt you, but in the end, it helps you. What he does may seem painful to you, but in the end, you'll thank him for doing it because it was for your good.

A really good friend doesn't agree with you all the time. No matter how brutally you roar, a good friend will stand right up in your face and say, "You're still wrong."

You don't have real help until you have someone who will confront you about what needs to be changed in your life.

God comes to each one of us . . .

To stand up to us, and to force us to face our sin.

To confront us about our lies.

To make us uncomfortable about our bad habits.

To move us away from mediocrity.

To challenge us to excellence.

Are you ready today for your private appointment with God?

Why God Chooses to Wrestle With You

God wrestles with you so that you will discover what you are made of. He already knows what He created you to be and He knows what you've done with His creation. He's waiting for you to discover who you are. He wrestles with you so you will know His power and your weakness, His wisdom and your error, His strength and your frailty.

God wrestles with you to make you realize that you are wasting your life . . .

that you are mistreating your wife . . .

that you aren't the "greatest" or the center of the universe . . .

that you aren't the "least" and unworthy of anything good.

God wrestles with you to make you see that you need to keep this job and not quit it like you did the last three jobs . . .

you need to stay involved with this church and not back away from it like you did the last three times you say that you "got religion" . . .

> Seek, and
> ye shall find.
> *(Matthew 7:7)*

you need to stay in your marriage and not wander off like you did the last time.

God wrestles with you until you face the facts of your life. He doesn't sugarcoat anything. He gives it to you straight. He wrestles with you until you admit . . .

Yes, I'm unstable.

Yes, I'm making excuses.

Yes, I was wrong.

God also wrestles with you so that you will start searching for Him and hunting for what He wants you to find.

Man is a hunter by nature. God's commands to man at his creation were to "be fruitful, and multiply, and replenish the earth, and subdue it: and have dominion . . . over every living thing that moveth upon the earth" (Genesis 1:28).

To subdue means to conquer; to have dominion means to maintain one's conquest. Somewhere as part of the masculine nature is the need to subdue, the need to conquer, the need to track down and bring something into dominion. There's a hunter inside every man.

We may be hunting for a contract or business deal.

We may be on the hunt for a woman.

We may be hunting for the perfect new car.

Sometimes we don't even really want what we are after, we are just hunting because it is our nature to hunt. Fishermen often catch fish, unhook them, and throw them right back. They say, "Look what I caught." And then they toss that fish back into the lake. That doesn't make the man any less a fisherman. It means that he is merely fishing for the sport of it, not for dinner. He is "hunting."

Unless we allow God to step in and give us the right goals and guide our "hunting" instinct, we can spend our entire life hunting for the wrong things.

Jesus said, "Seek ye *first* the kingdom of God" (Matthew 6:33). And He promised that if you seek for it, you'll find it. (See Matthew 7:7.)

Wrestle with God today until the night ends, the dawn breaks, and you can see His face, feel His love, and know His purpose.

The Urgency of God's Purpose

Return NOW.

There is always an urgency in God's call for us to repent of our sin and to return to Him.

There is also a persistence in God's wrestling with us. People will sometimes tell us what they think, but then they abandon us. God doesn't give up. He wrestles with us *until.* He isn't swayed from His purpose.

> Return ye now every man from his evil way, and amend your doings, and go not after other gods to serve them, and ye shall dwell in the land which I have given to you.
> *(Jeremiah 35:15)*

There's an appointed time for the wrestling match in your life to end. God wrestled with Jacob "until the breaking of the day" (Genesis 32:24). God wrestled with urgency, with insistency, with greater and greater strength. He knew that if Jacob didn't confront who he was in that night, he was going to miss the prime opportunity to become who he was destined to be.

You may be running out of time, too.

A lot of things you perhaps could get away with in times past . . . you no longer can get away with. A lot of excuses you've used in the past . . . you no longer will be allowed to use.

God's urgency must not be ignored. He knows something about your life and your encounter with Him that you don't know. He knows when Satan's assassins have been launched against you for your demise. He knows when the death angel is allowed to do his work. He knows when He is returning again.

Before you lose your life . . .

Before you lose your integrity . . .

Before you lose your wife . . .

Before you lose your son or daughter . . .

Before you lose your future blessing . . .

Before you lose what God has given to you . . .

God's urgency is for a purpose. Don't ignore Him.

You don't have time to fool around.

You don't have time for detours.

You don't have time for childish things.

You don't have time for your rebellion.

You don't have time to play games.

You don't have time for an affair.

You don't have time for meetings and committees that aren't important.

If you're going to experience the place God has reserved for you, you are probably going to have to cut off some relationships . . .

give up some things . . .

dig deeper into God's Word . . .

learn how to pray for yourself . . .

and truly become the priest of your home.

If people ask you why you can't do what you've done in the past, tell them, "I don't have time. I'm going someplace and I've got to get there."

Look at your watch right now and say to yourself, "Now is the appointed time for me to serve God so I can dwell in the land He has prepared for me!"

The Tomb
Is No
Place
To Live

The Reality of the Spirit Realm

There is a world about which many of us are unconscious, or unaware. It is real nonetheless. In fact, it is more real than the world we can see, touch, taste, hear, or feel. It is the realm of the spirit.

The most real part of you is your spirit. You *are* a spirit. Many men seem to think the real part of them is their body, but no matter how much you build it up, manicure it, dress it, or feed it, you are not first and foremost a body. You *have* a body. You live in a body. It is a temporary home.

You also have a soul. The soulish area of man is where most of the problems occur; this is the area of the mind, the emotions, memories, appetites, desires. The mind of man, including the mind of the Christian, is often trapped between the physical and the spiritual — flashbacks to memories of the former life in the flesh can fill the mind. The result can be a tremendous

We wrestle not against flesh and blood, but against principalities, against powers, against the rulers of the darkness of this world, against spiritual wickedness in high places.

(Ephesians 6:12)

wrestling match, with each force, spirit and flesh, trying to dominate the other. In fact, it is only when a man receives the Word of God and engrafts it to his mind that he is able to save his mind from the clutches of the flesh.

Demons are disembodied spirits. They don't have a body, and they don't have a soul — they have no mind of their own or will of their own. Their will is totally subjected to Satan. They are vessels and carriers of Satan's nature. They are filled with his desires, his lusts, his passions, and his unclean thoughts.

Because demons don't have bodies, they are seeking one. They are seeking a vehicle through which they can express their lusts and passions for evil.

Jesus once said to Simon Peter, "Simon, Simon, behold, Satan hath desired to *have* you, that he may sift you as wheat" (Luke 22:31). He was saying to Peter, "Satan desires to possess you, to have you, to dominate you." Men know what it means to lust after a woman in order to *have* her. That's the way Satan looked at Peter. He lusted after him, that he might completely *take* Peter's mind and body — to satisfy his cravings through him.

Satan's demons desire the same thing today regarding you —

To use your body, your temper, your lust, your passions.
To work through the broken places of your childhood

to fulfill their ravenous desires.
To possess you so that he might sift you.

Before Satan makes a move to have you, he studies you. He learns all he can about you — your moods,
> your attitudes,
>> your background,
>>> your past hurts and
>>>> painful memories,
>>>>> your desires.

He has stalked you. He has put you under surveillance, watching always for an opportunity to move in to take you. He *longs* to possess,
> dominate,
>> control,
>>> rule over,
>>>> and act through you.

That's the reason you must walk *closely* by the side of Jesus. Cling to Him. Never for a moment believe Satan's lie that you can go it alone or make it on your own strength. David — one of the bravest and most capable men who ever lived — cried out to God, "Hide me under the shadow of your wings." (See Psalm 17:8.) Tucked under the wings of God . . . that's the only place you will ever feel fully secure.

Trust in the Lord today. Ask Him to give
you the courage and faith to
withstand Satan's sifting.

Who Is in Control?

Every act of your life is motivated by a spiritual force.

Who is controlling you?

What is motivating you?

What spirit is being satisfied through your body?

If it is Satan's spirit that you are allowing to work in you — manifest through his demons — then you are grieving the Holy Spirit. Anytime you allow the enemy to work his will through your mind or body, you grieve the Holy Spirit.

> Lead us not into temptation, but deliver us from evil.
> *(Matthew 6:13)*

The Holy Spirit also desires to use you. But He wants to use you for God's glory and God's service. You will feel satisfied and have great joy when you live for God's glory. The Holy Spirit's purpose is not to dominate you or crush you, but to fulfill you.

Satan desires to use you for his own purpose, as a pawn in his hand to laugh in God's face. He desires to use you, abuse you, and then refuse you. You are in a state of living death when you succumb to the devil's purpose. He defies God as he works in you through his demons, saying in effect, "Is this someone You wanted, God? Well, I'm here first and I'm not moving. You called this man Your son? Look who's really in charge of his life. Look what I am making Your son do."

Temptation is Satan's tool for getting you to do things that you really don't want to do. Deep inside your spirit, you know that what he is tempting you to do is wrong. The worst and most hardened criminals in our world today know they have done wrong — they may blame others for their actions, they may act as if they don't care about the fact that they've done wrong, been caught, or are facing serious consequences — but deep inside, they know. They knew when they were doing wrong that what they were doing was wrong.

Satan's lie is that you have a *right* to do wrong.

Society is at fault. You have a right to get even with society.

Your daddy is at fault. You have a right to rebel against him.

Your boss is at fault. You have a right to steal from him or cheat him.

God is at fault. He made you this way. You have a right to act the way you do because He made you with this temper, this anger, this lust, this desire.

God's Word says that you have a right to choose. Joshua said to the Israelites, "Choose you this day whom ye will serve . . . as for me and my house, we will serve the LORD" (Joshua 24:15). You have a right to choose, a free will, a mind that can make a decision. But you have no right to sin.

Make sure today that you are yielding the control of your life *only* to God.

**Make it your prayer today:
"Deliver me from evil!"**

Don't Let Satan Divide and Conquer You

One of Satan's foremost tactics is the tactic of "divide and conquer." When Jesus encountered the man with an unclean spirit, He found him dwelling among the tombs. He was outside the city, away from family and friends. He had been "divided," and then conquered.

Satan always and relentlessly will attempt to move you away from community, family, and ministry. He will do anything in his power to convince you to break away, because he can conquer you more easily if you are isolated.

The enemy will move you to break away from others by feeding you lies, some of which are that . . .

You're exceptional. You're not really like these people. You are better than they are.

Your situation is different. You grew up in conditions that weren't like those of anybody else's.

Your childhood has molded you in certain ways that cannot be altered.

Your problem is unique. Nobody can relate to your problem because nobody has had it as bad as you had it. They can't relate to how you feel.

These lies become your excuses. They become your false premise for your taking license to act or speak in ways that are contrary to God's commandments. If you think that you aren't like other people, then it's only one step further for you to come to the conclusion that you don't have to abide by the same rules as other people.

If you find yourself saying . . .

I wouldn't be like this if my mother hadn't given me away . . .

> *if I'd had a different father . . .*
>
> > *if I had a more loving wife . . .*
> >
> > > *if I had a better job . . .*
> > >
> > > > *if I had not faced so much opposition . . .*

. . . wake up! You are giving yourself a passport to failure, a visa to flunk. You are hardening your attitude so that no matter who preaches to you, you whip out your yeah-but card and say, "This is why your message won't work for me."

If you adopt an attitude that you are "different," then you mentally and emotionally begin to separate yourself from other people. You disconnect from your foundation and from the fundamentals of truth. There's grave danger in that, especially if you are disconnecting from people who truly know God and are serving Him.

Once you are disconnected mentally and emotionally, you are also disconnected in other areas of your life whether you intended to be or not. You'll find it impossible to keep a job . . .

hold a marriage together . . .

relate in good ways to your children . . .

or make any long-term commitment that requires self-discipline.

The reason that you offer to others is always a *good* reason. It makes sense to you. It may even make sense to other people. It just doesn't fly with God.

Your excuse may keep you from being disgraced. But it will also keep you from being convicted and from changing.

Don't buy into Satan's lies. Don't give yourself license to lay in the cesspool of sin. Get rid of your excuses!

Refuse to be separated from God's people, God's plan for righteousness, or God's purpose for your life.

When Satan comes around with his lies, confront him with God's truth.

Beware:
Man Out of Control

One of the indications that a person is bound by Satan's influence is that "no man could bind him, no, not with chains."

The issue is one of control.

Now, I'm not talking about whether this man was possessed or oppressed. In either case, a person is being controlled by Satan. Even a Christian can be so oppressed that he operates under Satan's control.

A little boy might be sitting on his daddy's shoulders, pulling at his left ear and saying, "Daddy, go this way," and then pulling at his right ear and saying, "Daddy, go that way." And in play, the daddy does what the little boy demands. This little boy isn't *in* his father, but he is *controlling* his father's actions. And that's the way demons operate. They seek to fuel our desires and direct our passions, and in so doing, exert such tremendous influence on our behavior that it's almost as if we no longer have a will of our own.

You can be so oppressed that you might as well be possessed. The result is that you are a lascivious man.

> There met him out of the tombs a man with an unclean spirit . . . no man could bind him, no, not with chains.
>
> *(Mark 5:2,3)*

Lasciviousness is unrestrained action. It is being "out of control." No limitations. Whatever flesh says, flesh gets.

If you are angry, you tear up everything in the house.

If you are lustful, you'll even try to date your sister-in-law.

If you are filled with hate, you'll break every stick of furniture in sight.

The man who is lascivious might as well wear a sign around his neck, "Man out of control." He does things he may not even like to do solely because they are *possible* to do. He can't be trusted. He can't fulfill responsibility.

The lascivious man can't be bound. He doesn't pay any attention to the restraints of others or to the normal conventions of society or to the normal restraints of his own conscience. He certainly doesn't pay any attention to the commandments of God.

Domestic violence is "man out of control." It's a man beating what he ought to be protecting, it's a man beating his own body.

Sexual and physical abuse is "man out of control." It's a man turning on his own *zera*, his seed, so that his own children can't feel comfortable sitting on his lap.

Lasciviousness knows no boundaries. It infects every race, every culture, every nation. Rich and poor. Educated and uneducated. It doesn't care if a man is wearing a pin-stripe suit with a red paisley tie or a plaid flannel shirt and jeans or a torn T-shirt and baggy pants.

Nobody tries to get close to a man out of control. They want to, but they are afraid to.

Daddy's drinking.

Papa's high.

Father's in a bad mood tonight.

Honey's not at home and it's midnight.

It's not a matter of temptation. All men are tempted. It's a matter of self-control and self-discipline. Can God trust you to control your own *self*, to put boundaries on yourself?

One of the indications that this man had an unclean spirit was that nobody could get him to stop doing what he was doing. And what is it that he was doing? He was "crying, and cutting himself with stones." He was hurting *himself*.

The Bible says this man "had been often bound with fetters and chains, and the chains had been plucked asunder by him, and the fetters broken in pieces: neither could any man tame him" (Mark 5:4).

This man had been caught in the past, but he got away. He had made New Year's resolutions, but he broke his commitment to himself before January was over. He had been to the altar before and told God, "never again," but he had lied to God. He had done the very thing he had vowed never to do again. And you know, once a person has lied to God, he has no trouble at all lying to his wife, his children, his pastor, his friend, his boss.

Oh, you're so slick. You can slip past anybody if you want to. You can get away with anything.

Oh, you're so discreet. You're just sitting idly by, hunting with your eyes. Nobody knows what you're thinking, nobody knows the fantasies that you are living out in your mind.

Oh, you're so clever. You have a justification for everything, an excuse for every action, an alibi for every hour.

The reality is, you are hurting yourself when you break through all barriers. You are cutting short your own potential. You are breaking chains that were in place for your own good.

Is there an area of your life today that is out of control? Ask God to bind it up — and to give you restraint by the power of the Holy Spirit.

Say no to your flesh today and say yes to the Spirit of God.

Stop Living in the Tombs

The fact is, we're killing ourselves. Countless men are living in the "tombs."

I'm not talking about murder in the streets. That's there, and it's real, but that's the "outer world." I'm talking about the "inner world," the world that's just behind the facade that you put on.

You can kill a person with your words, your attitude, your absence. You can kill a relationship without any other weapon than your tongue. You can murder an association or a relationship without exploding any bomb; you can destroy it by neglect.

We are a people living out in the tombs. We're surrounded by death, and much of it is death that we have inflicted upon ourselves.

How many aborted babies were yours, and you didn't even know it because you weren't *around* to know it?

How many of those boys in the 'hood are running in gangs because you refused to be a father to them, and perhaps didn't even know you *were* their father?

How many women are in counseling offices every week because of what you said you'd do that you didn't do, or because of what you said you didn't do that you did do?

How many chains have you broken?

How many people are bleeding from wounds that you inflicted?

How many of your children are going to need serious pastoral counseling?

How many people are suicidal or messed up in their minds because of the lies you told?

How much death and destruction have you caused in your life? What tombs are you living in?

Jesus said, "I am the way, the truth, and the life" (John 14:6). Turn to Jesus today and ask Him to forgive you for all the deaths you have caused. Ask Him to lead you into the FULLNESS of His life.

Today can be your resurrection day in Christ Jesus!

The Victims of Spiritual AIDS

$\text{A}_{\text{IDS.}}$

It's a deadly disease.

But there's something even worse than acquired immune deficiency syndrome and it's this: "Spiritual AIDS."

A spiritually acquired immune deficiency syndrome has some of the same hallmarks as AIDS:

> This poor man cried, and the LORD heard him, and saved him out of all his troubles.
>
> *(Psalm 34:6)*

- It is *acquired.* You get it, catch it, or buy it. You become infected with it. You pick it up and it stays in you.

- Its presence in you is related to the broken-down barriers in your life. Just as your immune system keeps you from becoming sick from every germ or virus or bug that comes close to you, so your *spiritual immune system* keeps you from falling prey to every trick and temptation of the enemy. When your immune system breaks down, you get sick. When your spiritual immune system breaks down, you are an easy target for the devil.

• It is a *deficiency*. You are lacking the spiritual immune system you are supposed to have. The barriers that once kept you from sin have been torn down in your mind. You know, people sometimes say they are scared to be around people with AIDS. The reality is, people with AIDS should be a lot more scared of you, a person without AIDS, than you should ever be of them. Why? Because you have immunity and they do not. You are carrying germs and viruses in your body that aren't affecting you because of your healthy immune system, but those germs and viruses can be deadly to them.

The person with spiritual AIDS catches everything that passes by him. The Bible says, "He that hath no rule over his own spirit is like a city that is broken down, and without walls." (Proverbs 25:28) Without immunity, without defense, without walls.

• It is a *syndrome*. Spiritual AIDS becomes a habit. It sets itself up in the spirit and it becomes a man's identity.

The man with an unclean spirit had a spiritual disease that was out of control, and it was killing him. He was already living in the tombs. He wasn't far from death himself.

The man with AIDS is a man who is living with a time bomb in his body. Death is stalking him. The man with spiritual AIDS is also living in a state of death — and his state is much worse because it is a state of *eternal* death.

The cure for spiritual AIDS is found in Psalm 34:14,17 — "Depart from evil, and do good; seek peace, and pursue it. . . . The righteous cry, and the LORD heareth, and delivereth them out of all their troubles."

Ask God to give a boost to your spiritual immune system today.

Hungering for Righteousness

The man with an unclean spirit looked strong. He caused fear in others. Nobody wanted to get close to him because they were afraid of his strength that could "pluck asunder" fetters and leave chains in pieces.

But when this man was alone, he was anything but strong. He was crying. (See Mark 5:4,5.)

Countless men are crying today because deep down inside their hearts, they have become something they didn't *want* to become.

Not wanting to be who you are is the key to your deliverance. It's not what you've *done* that makes you a candidate for God's forgiveness; it's how you *feel* about what you have done and how you *feel* about what you want to be.

Jesus did not cross the Sea of Galilee on a stormy night to meet this man simply because he had an unclean spirit. No doubt there were people with an unclean spirit on the shore where Jesus was. No . . . Jesus was led by God to this man because this man was in the tombs "crying." He didn't want to be the man he had become. He didn't want his future to be the same as his past.

Thank goodness, Jesus didn't say, "Blessed is he who *IS* righteousness." That would eliminate all of us from God's blessing! Thank goodness, Jesus said, "Blessed is he who still wants to be righteous — who still has an appetite for doing the right thing, who still thirsts to be a better person, who still wants to be whole even though he knows he isn't whole . . .

who still wants to be the good husband he knows he isn't . . .

who still wants to be the father he

believes he can be but isn't right now . . .

who still wants to change and grow,

who still desires to be holy."

Deliverance begins with desire, a PASSION in you that challenges the PROBLEM in you.

I do not want to live like this anymore.

I do not want to be like this.

I do not want to act like this.

I do not want to be a drunk, a drug addict, a homosexual.

I do not want to be this angry, this critical, this cold, this indifferent, this destructive, this lazy, this trite.

I do not want to be jealous, suspicious, or distant.

What is it that you *don't* want to BE anymore?

What is it that you *don't* want to DO anymore?

What is your cry to God?

God can and does hear you when you cry. He doesn't condemn you for crying out to Him. Rather, He moves toward you when you cry. He comes to you with deliverance and forgiveness.

**Cry out to God today for the
changes you want in YOUR life.**

Stop Cutting Yourself Down

This man with an unclean spirit is a classic example of a man with extremely low self-esteem. He didn't value himself. He was cutting his own flesh with stones.

Countless men today are "cutting themselves" in their own minds. They may put on a brave front to the outside world, but when they are alone, they wound themselves and bleed — they dissipate their own energy, their own life force.

> He was . . . in the tombs . . . cutting himself with stones.
>
> *(Mark 5:5)*

They are insecure about themselves, hating themselves. The man who hates himself cannot love another person. How can you give to another person what you can't even give to yourself? It's not possible. The man with low self-esteem can't build up other people — not his wife, or his children, or his employees, or those he is asked to supervise at work.

Self-image is the most important thing in the world that you need to have next to your faith in God. It doesn't matter what others think of you. It matters only what *you* think of you based upon what *God* thinks of you.

When you start cutting and gnashing at yourself, you become preoccupied with self-hatred.

We each treat other people out of our own reservoir of self-dignity and self-respect. If you don't have respect for yourself, you won't have genuine respect for other people. Jesus taught, "Love thy neighbour as thyself" (Matthew 19:19). If you don't love yourself, you can't love your neighbor.

The Bible also says that a man should love his own wife as he loves himself. (See Ephesians 5:28.) If you don't like yourself, you can't love your wife.

Most men who abuse their wives are self-haters. It is out of their own anger and frustration that they lash out at their wives. They aren't overflowing with hatred for their wives, but for them*selves*. If you truly want to know how you feel about your*self*, look at how you treat your wife. She is your body, one with you. She is "bone of your bone and flesh of your flesh" — the feminine expression of your masculinity. The way you treat your wife is the way you treat your*self*.

If you are physically, sexually, emotionally, or verbally abusing your wife, you are abusing yourself.

You are denying,

screaming at,

lashing out at,

ignoring in your silence,

> cutting to the core of . . .
> *your very own self.*

You cannot receive the esteem of your son or daughter if you do not esteem yourself.

The man with an unclean spirit was cutting himself, doing far more damage to himself than any other person had ever been able to do to him. The same holds true for us. We do far more damage to ourselves than others do.

Self-esteem has to come from self. You won't believe the good things that anybody else says about you unless you first believe those things about yourself.

I like me. I'm glad if other people like me, but I don't do what I do *so* that other people will like me. I'm not dependent upon whether other people like me or not.

If I come across anybody who doesn't like me, I am very happy to say to them, "I disagree with you." I don't give in to the way they feel about me and like myself less. I simply disagree with their opinion. I like me! I have a right to my own opinion.

I know all about me . . . and I still like me. I know all my faults, but I still like me.

I like me in part because I'm still here — I've survived. I've lost some friends, some jobs, some cars, some things . . . but I'm here. If you have no other reason to like yourself other than the fact that you are a survivor of life's problems, like yourself for that reason.

Be who you are and be proud of it.

Not a lot of blacks live in West Virginia, especially in the rural areas. Sometimes when I was out in the remote regions, I encountered little white children who had never seen a black man. I recall this one little boy who just stared at me, aghast. He had never seen anything like me in his life. He said, "Lord, mister. Are you that color all over?"

His mother almost turned purple in embarrassment. I said to him, "Yes, I think I am. Everywhere I can see and everywhere I can see in the mirror, I'm this color. It seems to be all over me."

I'm not at all ashamed of being a black man. That's who God made me to be!

Start believing in the *you* that God made *you* to be. He loves you and that's all the reason you need for loving yourself.

**Compliment God today on the fine job
He did when He made you.**

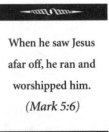

Worship Away Your Problem

This man with an unclean spirit saw Jesus from afar off and his response was to worship Him.

I want you to note that this man didn't get delivered first and then worship Jesus. He worshiped Jesus and *then* was delivered by Jesus.

Some men today aren't delivered from the oppression they are experiencing from the devil because they haven't learned how to *worship away their problems.*

> When he saw Jesus afar off, he ran and worshipped him.
>
> *(Mark 5:6)*

Even the devil has to bow down and acknowledge that Jesus is Lord of all. The Bible tells us that *every* knee must bow to Him: "of things in heaven, and things in earth, and things under the earth; and that every tongue should confess that Jesus Christ is Lord, to the glory of God the Father"(Philippians 2:10,11). Every system, government, and society must bow to the Lord of lords and King of kings.

Every hex, every curse, every evil work must BOW to the name of Jesus. That includes every satanic power and generational curse. "No weapon that is formed against thee shall prosper; and every tongue that shall rise against thee in judgment thou shalt condemn. This is the heritage of the servants of the LORD, and their righteousness is of me, saith the LORD" (Isaiah 54:17).

Your childhood hurts . . .

your painful memories . . .

your addiction . . .

your past sins . . .

must BOW to the name of Jesus. You must condemn anything that rises up in you to destroy you and your ministry — your lust, your anger, your hate, your bitterness, your rebellious spirit, your job-quitting, church-hopping spirit — and say to it, "*BOW* to the name of Jesus."

Bow in worship.

When this man began to worship Jesus, the demons in him cried out, "What have I to do with thee, Jesus, thou Son of the most high God? I adjure thee by God, that thou torment me not" (Mark 5:7).

The fact is, demons have NOTHING to do with Jesus. They have nothing in common with Him, no association with Him, no alliance with Him. And Jesus has NOTHING to do with them except to cast them out. The very presence of Jesus torments demons.

If you are in a truly anointed worship service, demons scream out and flee from people who are calling out to the name of Jesus. Nobody has to touch a person or pray a long prayer over a person with unclean spirits. The very atmosphere of worship is a torment to demon powers.

Worship is the key to your deliverance.

Run to Jesus today and worship Him!

Breaking the Devil's Stronghold

avid was a good man. He was creative, strong, courageous. He was a man of musical and songwriting talent. He was a natural leader. But he had a generational curse on his life — a lust problem that cropped up from time to time.

Everybody around David apparently knew he had this problem. In fact, the Bible says that when David was an old man and he could not get warm, his servants brought a young virgin to lie in his bosom, that "the king may get heat." (See 1 Kings 1:1,2.) His servants said, in effect, "If being with this young woman can't get David's circulation going, nothing can! He probably *is* dying if he doesn't feel anything when he's with her."

The generational sin in David was passed on to Amnon, who had a lustful spirit for his sister, Tamar. He lured her to his bed and raped her. The Bible tells us that when David heard what Amnon had done to Tamar, he was very angry . . . but he didn't say or do anything to Amnon. What could he say? His son was just like him. His own spirit of lust had passed on to his son. (See 2 Samuel 13.)

Lust is not a craving,
a fancy,
or a whim. It's sin.

When a pattern of evil passes from generation to generation, it becomes what the Bible calls a spiritual "stronghold." A spirit of evil is passed from generation to generation until it truly has a *strong hold* on a man's life. He can't get free of it simply because he wishes to be free or hopes to be free. Only Jesus can set that man free.

Many men can look back at their family history and see a bad spirit at work in their family, generation after generation.

Daddy drank too much . . . and granddaddy drank too much . . . and great-granddaddy drank too much.

Dad cheated on Mom, and Grandpa cheated on Grandma, and Great-Grandpa wasn't even around to cheat on Great-Grandma.

Father had a bad temper . . . and so did grandfather . . . and so did great-grandfather.

Sometimes a man can look and see a pattern of abuse and sin and evil coming at him from both sides of his family tree. It isn't only his grandpa on his father's side who was filled with anger, but his grandpa on his mother's side. Or, a man may know nothing about his grandparents or great-grandparents — and perhaps not even his father's behavior — but he may see a particular pattern of behavior rampant among his brothers, uncles, and cousins. His *family* has been infected with a bad spirit.

When Jesus commanded the demon who afflicted the man in the tombs to tell Him his name, the demon replied, "Legion: for we are many" (Mark 5:9).

Very often, the demonic oppression on our lives has many facets — it has many names, simultaneously. The spirit is not just one of lust, but of anger. It is one of emotional deprivation and one of poverty. When you combine various types of demonic oppression they multiply in their hold on a person's life.

A spiritual stronghold is not something that you can drink out of your life . . .

smoke out of your life . . .

curse out of your life . . .

argue out of your life . . .

or plead out of your life. BUT you can CAST it out of your life!

Before you go to the judge . . .

Before you go to the rehab center . . .

Before you go to the counselor . . .

Go to God.

Get to the altar and ask God to break that stronghold from your life. You may still need help to learn *how* to express yourself, but first and foremost, you need God's help in breaking the spiritual oppression that has you in its clutches.

If you don't break the spiritual strongholds on your life, your own sons and daughters will be victims of it. Lay your hand on your son and your daughter and say . . .

Don't let the same things that infected me, infect another generation.

Don't let the same abuse be passed on to my children.

You could be a great husband.

You could be a great father.

You could be an outstanding employee.

You could be a very effective witness.

What keeps you from it? Name that stronghold and ask God to break it off your life.

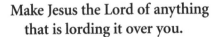

Make Jesus the Lord of anything
that is lording it over you.

Breaking the Curse of Poverty Off Your Life

J ust recently I heard a report about a young child who went to school wearing a $400 pair of shoes. This child was the son of a woman who was selling drugs. I thought to myself, if that woman can trust the devil and his demons to clothe her baby like that, how is it that Christian men refuse to trust God to take care of them and their families.

And yet I see it all the time: Christian men jealous of other men. Mostly they are jealous of their *stuff*. They are jealous of their house, or their car, or their wristwatch, or their clothes, or their gold jewelry, or some other possession they have.

Then, to compound matters, they try to cover up and justify their jealousy by saying, "We shouldn't have nice things or own the best that is

> Bring ye all the tithes into the storehouse, that there may be meat in mine house, and prove me now herewith, saith the LORD of hosts, if I will not open you the windows of heaven, and pour you out a blessing, that there shall not be room enough to receive it. And I will rebuke the devourer for your sakes, and he shall not destroy the fruits of your ground; neither shall your vine cast her fruit before the time in the field, saith the LORD of hosts. *(Malachi 3:10,11)*

available to purchase." They turn their jealousy into a stingy, angry spirit. They complain about the kind of car their pastor drives, although when they were in sin, they never once complained about the gold jewelry and big diamond rings and fancy cars that were owned by the man who ran the local bar or the corner pool hall.

I refuse to give in to the jealousy of other people. I want to say to any person who might be jealous of something I own, "I paid for what I have, and I paid first of all in the spirit realm."

God said that He would bless me if I brought my tithes into His storehouse. He said He would open up the windows of heaven and pour out a blessing on me and my family that was so great I wouldn't have room enough to receive it. He said He would rebuke the devourer from my family. He would cause us to be fruitful in every area and that others would see our blessing and call us "delightsome." (See Malachi 3:12.)

I broke the spirit of poverty over my house by giving my tithes and giving my offerings. I beat the devil out of my checkbook and pleaded the blood over my finances. I scraped and crawled my way up out of poverty and into God's prosperity by doing what God said to do! And you can, too.

I refuse to listen to those who have spent the money that should have been their tithe and offering to God, who are bound up in a spirit of poverty and stinginess toward the things of God, and then complain that I shouldn't receive or enjoy God's blessings. The simple fact is, I have done what God has said to do. They haven't.

Do what God says to do in His Word. And then . . . Let God bless you! Enjoy what He gives to you!

Take authority over your finances today. Rebuke the devil from your finances in the name of Jesus, give your tithes and offerings — as the man and priest of your house, and then look for God's blessings to be poured out from heaven on you.

Casting the Devil Out of Your Family

Jesus' response to the man who was living in the tombs was to speak to the evil spirit in him, "Come out of him." (See Mark 5:8.) Jesus didn't condemn the man. He condemned the evil spirit that had attached itself to the man.

This was a good man who had a very bad spirit in him. The bad spirit needed to be pulled out of him, the power of the evil spirit broken in his life.

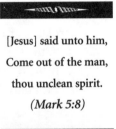

[Jesus] said unto him, Come out of the man, thou unclean spirit.

(Mark 5:8)

When Jesus rebuked the devil in this man's life, the demon started pleading. He didn't plead about leaving the man, but about leaving the "neighborhood." It was as if he was saying to Jesus, "I've been assigned to this territory. Don't make me leave my post."

The devil may not mind your being free. But he will mind being cast out of your family. He may say, "If I can't have you, at least let me have your son." The devil will do his best to drive a wedge between you and your son so you can't communicate and so that he will come to a conclusion that you don't love him.

The devil may say, "Fine, if I can't have you. Let me have your brother, your cousin, your neighbor." He wants to stay in your neighborhood.

Your answer to his compromise must always be NO!

Shout it at him. Refuse to give an inch. NO to his having your son. NO to his having your daughter. NO to his having your brother or sister. NO to his having your neighbor. Shout it *LOUD*.

There was so much demonic power in this one man that when Jesus commanded the power to leave, He sent it into an entire herd of swine. They broke their natural instinctual tendency and leaped into the sea.

If the devil can't have you, he will make a bid for your family. Don't allow it.

Pray that the blood of Jesus will cover your entire family today. Claim your wife, your children, your brothers and sisters, your nieces and nephews, and your grandchildren for God.

Directing Your Deliverance Back Home

When a man is truly delivered by Jesus, everybody can tell. You can't keep it a secret.

When the man with an unclean spirit named Legion was delivered, everybody in both the city and the surrounding countryside knew it. They all went out to see what had happened.

When you are delivered by God . . .

Your old girlfriends are going to know it.

So are your old running buddies.

And your old drinking buddies.

And your coworkers.

The people in your old neighborhood are going to hear about it.

And for some of you, the people in your church will be able to see a difference!

Don't be ashamed to be a witness!

Be happy about what God has done for you.

> And when he was come into the ship, he that had been possessed with the devil prayed him that he might be with him. Howbeit Jesus suffered him not, but saith unto him, Go home to thy friends, and tell them how great things the Lord hath done for thee, and hath had compassion on thee. And he departed, and began to publish in Decapolis how great things Jesus had done for him: and all men did marvel.
> *(Mark 5:18-20)*

If all God wanted was your salvation, He would have heard your pleas for forgiveness, saved you, and then killed you. No! God wants you to be His witness.

Where?

First, to those who are right where you are.

This man wanted to go with Jesus as He departed by boat to go to the other side of the lake, but Jesus said no. Why? He intended for this man to be a witness *to the people who knew him best.*

His ministry wasn't to be in the tombs or in the mountains where he had withdrawn in his torment. It was to be in the cities of the Decapolis, the place no doubt where this man had first become oppressed by evil.

God never intends for us to live apart from the world, but to be witnesses *to* the world.

Have you ever been to a meeting or a conference that was so wonderful, you never wanted it to end? Have you ever been on a retreat in a place so beautiful that you never wanted to go home?

That's the way the unclean man felt after Jesus had delivered him from the demon power that was oppressing him. He didn't want to leave Jesus' presence.

God frequently gives us "mountaintop" spiritual experiences — leading us to times and places where we can experience a powerful anointing of His presence — but then the time comes when He says to us, just as Jesus said to this man, "Go home."

Ask God today where He wants you to witness for Him. It very likely will be the place you know best.

Today, tell somebody who is CLOSE to you about the love and power of God.

Getting Back Into Your Right Mind

When God does a work in your life, He does it in calmness. He brings about a peace in your life. All hell may be breaking out against you, but you can sit back and whistle.

This man with an unclean spirit sat calmly at Jesus' feet after his deliverance. He had been ranting and raving, roaming through the mountains and tombs — restless in his outward actions, just as he was forever restless in his inner spirit. After his deliverance by Jesus, he knew the peace that only God can give.

[They saw him] that was possessed with the devil, and had the legion, sitting, and clothed, and in his right mind ....

(Mark 5:15)

This man was clothed, where he once had been naked. The Bible tells us that those who overcome the enemy shall "be clothed in white raiment" — they will be in God's eyes as if they have never sinned. Peter tells us that we are to be "clothed with humility," completely submissive to God so that we will hear what God wants us to hear, see what God wants us to see, and then say and do what God wants us to say and do. (See Revelation 3:5 and 1 Peter 5:5.)

Have you thought about the fact that once this man had been delivered and forgiven by Jesus, it was as if he had *never* been under the influence of a demon power named Legion? It was as if he had never walked around with torn chains hanging from his arms and legs, slashing himself with stones and living in the tombs. He was *clothed* with righteousness. God saw him only as *forgiven.* He had no "past" with God, only a bright future.

The assurance of forgiveness is what gives a man peace. When you truly know you are forgiven, you feel a calmness born of trust, a peace born of assurance. Paul described it for the Philippians as a peace that "passeth all understanding" (Philippians 4:7).

Every man I know needs this kind of peace.

You cannot be the head of your house and be hysterical at the same time. You can't fall apart just because your wife has fallen apart. You can't lose your cool just because your kids have lost theirs. Somebody has to keep their wits about them and say, "We're going to come out of this." As priest of your home, you are called to be a stabilizing, protecting force in your home. When you walk in the front door of your house, everybody in your family should feel safer. You are called by God to have a "right mind." "Let this mind be in you, which was also in Christ Jesus" (Philippians 2:5).

Having a right mind means being aware of your responsibilities and accepting them.

I know many men who let their wives deal with all the stress of the family, including anxiety over the family finances, worries over the spiritual life of each family member, and concerns over family provision. That's not her role. You and your wife must share the responsibility for your children and work together to make a plan for your family. It's a cop-out for a man to say to his children every time they ask for a decision, "Go ask your mama."

Can you answer these questions about your children?
Where are your children?
What time do they go to school?
What time do they get home?
Where are they in the evenings?
What time will they be back?
You should know!

Having a right mind means being responsible in providing for your family.

I see absolutely no excuse today for a man not to have a job. If there isn't a job available in your community that's suited to your educational level, find a job that's lower than your educational level and fill it until a better job opens up. If it's not illegal, and it's not sin, go for it! Pick up a shovel and dig a ditch if you have to. You may say, "Bishop, have you ever done that?" I certainly have. I have dug ditches until my hands were bleeding in order to get $100 to buy groceries to feed the children for another week. As long as I am in my house, I am responsible for providing for my household.

If you can't provide everything you *want* to provide for your family, do what you *can* do. You may not know everything, but you can find people who can teach your children the things necessary for them to know. You may not understand the Bible fully, but you can get your children to church and Sunday school and to youth group programs where they can learn the Bible, experience the power of God, and learn how to apply the truth of God to their lives. You may not know everything about prayer, but you can pray for your children with a humility of heart and a love that speaks volumes.

Ask the Lord to transform you by the renewing of your mind. (See Romans 12:2.) The Lord Jesus Christ *is* your sanity.

Ask God to give you a clear, pure, right mind today.

Guard, Gird, and Guide

As husband and father, your role is threefold:
- *to guard your family,* which includes practical safety, but also spiritually guarding against evil.

- *to gird your family,* which means to provide for your family the support it needs — including food, shelter, clothing, and general well-being.
- *to guide your family,* which includes having a plan and direction for your family — setting goals, developing your family's witness and outreach efforts, and guiding your family into a greater understanding of God's truth.

Guarding means that if there's a strange noise in the night, *you* get up. If your child is having serious trouble in school, *you* go there. If somebody comes to the door, *you* answer it. Guarding sometimes means simply showing up. For you to be there when your child needs you, you need to be sensitive to their needs.

Girding means that your children have shoes on their feet and clothes on their back. It means making sure your wife has what she needs. I do everything in my power to make sure my wife looks good. She's a reflection on me! I do everything I can to make sure that she's happy and content. She's my best sermon! In fact, I expect to live in such a way with my wife that if I die before she does and she remarries, her next husband will *hate* me. He'll have to work overtime to do for her as much as I have done — including writing songs and poetry just for her, blowing kisses to her across the room, buying her nice things, giving her the compliments she deserves. He's going to get very tired taking care of her in the way that she is accustomed to.

Guiding means having a plan. For example, as you face your family's finances, do so with a plan. Then, share that plan with your family. Make it an all-family effort. Say to your wife and children, "Things are tight right now, but here's what we are going to do. In three months, this is where we should be. In a year, this is our goal. In three years, we should have our finances fully under control." Give your children a future to anticipate with hope. They can't have hope if you haven't spelled out a plan and set a direction toward a circumstance that will be better than what they know today.

Have an agenda for your family's spiritual growth. Plan with your wife what you are going to do together to raise your children up to know and love God, His Word, and His church.

Guard.

Gird.

Guide.

Make that your motto!

Even as you choose to guard, gird, and guide your family, trust God to guard, gird, and guide YOU.

Getting to Jesus . . . No Matter What It takes!

The Untapped Power of Christine

One of the things that needs to be better understood within the Body of Christ is the power of Christ. In many cases, the Church needs to understand this as much as the world does. Christ is not a weak, impotent, unresponsive force. Our God is a God of power — He impacts every situation and circumstance He is allowed to enter with revolutionary, life-changing power.

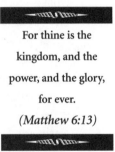

For thine is the kingdom, and the power, and the glory, for ever.

(Matthew 6:13)

One Christian can chase a thousand, and two can chase ten thousand because our God allows it to be so. (See Deuteronomy 32:30.) The Church bears all the power necessary to heal marriages and to heal those who are sick — physically, emotionally, mentally, and spiritually. The real psychologist's couch resides in the Word of God. The Church can impact every community — its families, its economy, its health.

When Jesus came to a city, the magistrates and all of the city leaders knew it. He worked in such a way that everybody knew He was there. He *changed* things.

It's time that more of us in the Body of Christ be noisier about the power of Christ — to be movers and shakers who will go into the enemy's camp and take back what he has stolen from us.

We have the answer to domestic violence, racial tension, immorality. His name is Jesus. We don't need to look to the White House, but to the Church house. We don't need to take over the ballot box; we need to kneel before the altar.

This is not to say that the Church today is so perfect that it couldn't be amended or improved. But what is wrong with the Church is of man, not Christ. His power is absolute, unchanging, and perfect.

The power of Christ can be criticized . . . but not contained. It can be frustrated or thwarted . . . but not stopped. It can be hindered . . . but not quenched. If God is behind even the smallest thing, it becomes mighty, effective, and powerful to the tearing down of all types of strongholds.

It's time we used the name of Jesus to declare that the enemy no longer has any authority over our own lives, or the lives of our families. We must force the issue with the enemy. We must be radical enough to "make" him loose us and let us go.

Say to the enemy today, "In the name of Jesus, loose me. Loose my family. We belong to God and to Him alone!"

Making a "Noise" and a Difference

When Jesus arrived in Capernaum, He turned the city upside down.

Whatever you enter today...
Whatever you belong to...
Whatever you participate in...
Whatever you are in...

Your presence ought to be felt.

If you're on the usher board, every usher ought to be blessed because you're on the board.

If you're on a neighborhood committee, every other person on the committee and every person your committee touches ought to be blessed because you are there.

> And again he entered into Capernaum... and it was noised that he was in the house.
>
> *(Mark 2:1)*

If you're on the job, your boss, your coworkers, your customers and clients, your vendors and suppliers, your employees ... everybody with whom you do business ought to be blessed. You are God's agent for making a difference for *good*.

Your presence also ought to provoke change. Wherever God is present, change happens. Things

187

grow. People's attitudes are altered. Situations are turned around. There's no way you can be filled with God's presence and then be incapable of altering your circumstances.

I recently was asked, "Bishop, what do you think about the hopelessness in our nation?" I said, "What hopelessness?" I don't believe in hopelessness. I believe that as long as you have a thumping of your heart in your chest, you should have hope. As long as you are a blip on a monitor and your skin is warm you *must* have hope! I don't care how bad you blew it or what you have done, as long as you can say, "Jesus," you have hope.

You have hope because you serve a God Who has the power to change things, and to call into being things that are not.

Make some noise today about Who God is and what God does. Do it by your love in action as much as by your words of hope!

**Be God's agent for change
wherever you go today.**

What Has You Bound?

This man who was sick of the palsy was in an immobile state. Palsy is a term that was applied to a number of diseases at the time of Jesus. It was used to describe the condition of any person who was unable to command movement in an area of his body. This man apparently was incapable of commanding movement that enabled him to walk.

Bringing one sick
of the palsy.
(Mark 2:3)

In palsy of this type, the muscles, tissues, blood vessels, bones, nerves, and every other physical attribute necessary for movement are present. But for some reason, flesh rebels against command.

I should be able to move from where I am, but I can't. I'm stuck.

I want to move on, but I can't. I'm stuck in this place.

I don't want to live like I'm living, but I can't seem to change. I'm stuck in this condition.

I want a better life for my family, but I can't seem to make it happen. I'm stuck where I am.

Men get angry when they feel "stuck." They feel as if everybody else is moving and free. They have all of the physical, mental, and emotional attributes necessary for change and growth — they can still think, still feel. They still have talents and skills. They still have opportunities and possibilities. But their inner spirit does not respond to command. They are in a state of inner rebellion.

Stress turns into pressure, and pressure into rage, and constant rage creates a state of weariness. Webster defines weary, in part, as having "your sense of pleasure exhausted." When you are weary, nothing is exciting. Everything seems bland. You become numb, unable to act or even to believe for change. Every day seems like the day before.

It doesn't matter if you live in a ghetto or a penthouse, if you are not liberated in your mind and encouraged in your spirit, you will feel as if you are in a jail cell. You will feel stress.

Stress, anger, and prejudice are not linked to any one race or level of income. They infect nearly every person. And if they become severe enough, they bring a person to a state of weariness, of numbness, of immobility.

Such a person is sick of inner palsy.

A man can get stuck in childhood memories.

He can get stuck in teenage issues.

He can get stuck in an adult problem.

While one type of palsy leaves a person "frozen," incapable of movement, another type of palsy leaves a person with spastic motions — the person can't coordinate his movements, or hold onto objects he desires to hold.

Some men can't hold a job.

They can't hold a relationship together.

They can't seem to hold onto their finances or save money.

They can't keep their word.

A part of their lives is out of control.

Lust out of control . . .

    rage out of control . . .

        bitterness out of control. The man with this type of palsy knows something is wrong with him, but he can't seem to do anything about it.

A third type of palsy comes from sheer muscle exhaustion. A man's muscles become so worn out he can't move. The mind, the emotions, and the spirit also can become exhausted.

If you have everyone around you drawing from you, you can quickly become depleted unless you have another means of making deposits into your life. That's true in your finances, your emotions, your ministry, your health. If you don't give something back to yourself, you will soon have nothing to give out. It simply isn't possible to be a continual encouragement to others, and not become discouraged, drained, or depleted in the process. You must avail yourself of conferences, meetings, seminars, and retreats that will build you up and give something back to your spirit.

Whatever the cause of this man's palsy — frozen muscles, spastic muscles, or exhausted muscles — Jesus was his Great Physician! Whatever your palsied state today, Jesus holds the key to your vibrancy, freedom, healing, and an abundant life.

The Bible tells us that when David's family was taken captive at Ziklag and David was "greatly distressed," he "encouraged himself in the LORD his God" (1 Samuel 30:6). Jude speaks of our "building up" ourselves on our most holy faith. How? By praying in the Holy Ghost and by keeping ourselves in the love of God, looking for the mercy of our Lord Jesus Christ unto eternal life. (See Jude 20,21.) Build yourself up in Jesus!

Refuse to live in a frozen, out of control, or exhausted state. Ask Jesus to impart to you His LIFE.

Be Prepared for a Heavy Load

Let me assure you of this, if you ever decide to carry another person, you will discover that he is heavy. It took four men to carry the man with palsy to Jesus and he no doubt was a heavy load for even four men to carry.

Anytime you pick up the weight — the problem, the need — of another person, you'll likely find that it is a heavy load. Don't ever be duped into thinking that ministry is easy. Genuine and effective ministry to another person is always a great challenge.

> They come unto him, bringing one sick of the palsy, which was borne of four.
>
> *(Mark 2:3)*

First, you must be sensitive to a person's need to be carried. In any church service you are in, there's somebody close to you who is lying on a "stretcher" on the inside. He may act as if he has his life together, but he knows he's putting on a facade. He knows he has a need, but he may have trouble telling you about it. He's hurting . . . he's out of control . . . he's paralyzed in some way . . . and he knows it. In all likelihood, his wife and children know. You will have to be very sensitive to the Holy Spirit if you are to know it, too.

Don't be fooled by the prayers he prays when others are listening. When he's alone, he's praying a different way.

He's mumbling and groaning and crying into his pillow. He's crying out, "Lord, if You don't help me, I'm going to lose everything I have."

Don't be fooled by his fancy clothes or big smile. On the inside he's crying, "Help!"

Don't be fooled by his race, his denomination, or his status in society.

Black man . . . gotta get to Jesus.

White man . . . gotta get to Jesus.

Brown man . . . gotta get to Jesus.

Red man . . . gotta get to Jesus.

Baptist man . . . gotta get to Jesus.

Pentecostal man . . . gotta get to Jesus.

Rich man . . . gotta get to Jesus.

Poor man . . . gotta get to Jesus.

Big-shot executive . . . gotta get to Jesus.

Down-and-outer . . . gotta get to Jesus.

Don't be put off by his "dirty" reputation or by his sin.

Man on crack . . . get him to Jesus.

Man abusing his wife . . . get him to Jesus.

Man abandoning his family . . . get him to Jesus.

Don't pick up another person only to drop him. If you commit to helping another person come to

Christ, make sure you bring him all the way to Jesus, no matter what it takes.

Many times we only want people delivered if it's easy on us. We don't want to have to sacrifice to see the deliverance or healing of another person.

Hold him steady.

Hold him tight.

Hold him until Jesus touches him with His power.

As you carry him, reassure him . . .

You have an appointment with a miracle. God has set a time for you to experience a complete makeover . . .

a massive turnaround . . .

a total reconstruction. You may not be able to help where you have been, but you can do something about where you are going. God has something better for you than anything you've known to this point!

Once you get a man to Jesus, you no longer have to carry him. Make sure you get him there, but once you have him in Jesus' presence, leave the work to Jesus. David said, "In thy presence is fulness of joy; at thy right hand there are pleasures for evermore" (Psalm 16:11).

If a person who is hurting is brought to Jesus, he isn't bashful about asking for what he needs. He knows that he may be experiencing his last chance to cry out to God and be heard. David cried out, "Lead me to the rock that is higher than I" (Psalm 61:2).

The hurting man WANTS you to take him to the One Who can meet his needs.

Helping another man get to Jesus is the greatest thing you can do in this world. Be a lifesaver, a soulwinner, a family-healer, a community-changer. It will happen as you get those with palsied spirits to Jesus, the Healer and Deliverer.

Join with a Christian friend today in praying and believing for a man who needs to be healed by Jesus. Be sensitive to what God tells you to do for him and say to him.

Bringing the Need to Jesus

These friends of the man with palsy brought him to Jesus. They didn't bring him to church — not to the bureaucratic power structure of the church or to a cold, dead church service. They brought him to the direct power of Jesus.

They brought him to the One Who could heal him. They brought him on a stretcher because he couldn't walk on his own power.

Every time I hold a men's conference, I know that there are some who come because they want to be "seen" at the conference . . .

others come because their friends are coming and

they don't want to be left out . . .

some come simply because they have a new suit and they are looking for a place to wear it . . .

still others come because they say they don't have anything better to do . . .

> And they come unto him. . . . And when they could not come nigh unto him for the press, they uncovered the roof where he was: and when they had broken it up, they let down the bed wherein the sick of the palsy lay.
> *(Mark 2:3,4)*

197

but there are also those who come on a stretcher. They may be brought by others who saw a need in their lives. They may be bringing their own needs into the conference as if bringing their inner man on a stretcher.

Those who have spiritual palsy — paralyzed in their need or sick with needs that are out of control — are the ones who get the most help. You see, they don't care if their names are called or who sits next to them. They are present to receive from Jesus all that He has for them. They need help . . . and they know it. They aren't embarrassed to reach out and receive all the help Jesus offers to them.

One of the things every person has to do in coming to Jesus is to get through the "press."

So many men come into the church today and they can't get to Jesus for the "press" — the press of all the church politics and the press of all the she-say, he-say, they-say hearsay. So many people are in their way, they can't see Jesus, even though He's the One they came to see and the One they need to see the most.

Some people have become so "professional" in their approach to church, they've forgotten why they are in the church. They've forgotten how they once felt, who they once were. They've lost sight of Jesus for the "press" of knowing who's hot and who's not. They've been around so long they've lost the pure motive of worship — of humbling and casting themselves before Jesus in total submission.

Don't let anything or anyone stand in the way of you bringing your need to Jesus.

Don't think about what other people might think of you . . . or what they might say to you. Don't worry about how you look . . . or about how you sound. The thing that matters is that you express yourself to God. Tell Him what you need. Praise Him for His provision.

No matter what effort it may take, get to Jesus today!

Expect to Receive

The men who brought their palsied friend to Jesus were men of faith. They didn't just have faith. They had an active, alive, relentless faith. They had faith in action.

I have to admit, I really LIKE the four men who were carrying the man with palsy to Jesus. They were not ordinary believers. They were *radical*. They weren't about to let anything get in the way of their receiving from Jesus what they wanted to receive. They had come to get a blessing and they weren't going home until they got it.

When Jesus saw their faith . . . .

(Mark 2:5)

When you go to church, make a commitment to yourself that you aren't going to go home until you have received from God what you need and want to receive from Him. Say to yourself . . .

I'm not going home until I come out of the bondage I'm in.

I'm not going home until I'm delivered from the pressure I feel.

I'm not going home until I get the blessing I need.

I'm not going home until I release the unforgiveness,

discouragement, anger, or resentment I feel.

Open yourself up to every bit of the power of Christ that is present.

Draw out the power of Christ that's in the singing.

In the preaching.

In the teaching.

In the praying.

In the communion.

In the giving.

In the loving.

Don't shut yourself off to any of the power of Christ that is flowing toward you.

And if there's no *power* of Christ Jesus in your church, get to a place where His power *is* flowing freely.

I have no use for dead churches. I have too many things that I'm fighting to come into a sophisticated arena where everybody is acting like intellectual, spiritual elitists and Holy Ghost yuppies. I need the power of God to be at work in my life every day!

I want to be in such powerful services that if I have any demons whatsoever trying to cling to me, the very power of praise and worship will shake them off. I want to be under the anointed preaching of God so that as the Word of God goes forth, it will deal with any issues in my heart that need to be changed. I need to be in the presence of an anointed ministry that will cause tears to well up in my eyes and confront me with the hard issues that I have been refusing to face, but need to face, so I can truly be set free of all influences of evil that are aimed at my destruction.

Go to where the power of God is being manifest. Open yourself to receive God's power and presence. Expect with your faith that God *will* fill you to overflowing.

Put your faith into action today.
Go to God and expect to
receive from Him.

Tear Away All Hindrances

When the four men who were carrying the palsied man arrived at the house where Jesus was preaching, they couldn't get in. They went up on the roof, but there was no opening there. They had to uncover the roof — peeling away the roofing material to create their own "door" through which they could let down their friend. Nothing about bringing this man to Jesus was easy. They had to make it happen.

The roof was a hindrance to them, but they didn't let a mere roof stop them.

What is hindering you today from getting to Jesus?

It might be your temper . . .

It might be your loneliness . . .

It might be your frustration . . .

It might be your childhood.

Tear the roof off! Get to Jesus — whatever it takes.

Who told you that you couldn't get a job?

Who told you that you couldn't have a good marriage?

> They uncovered the roof where he was: and when they had broken it up, they let down the bed wherein the sick of the palsy lay.
>
> *(Mark 2:4)*

Who told you that you couldn't get free of drugs? *Tear the roof off! Believe God can do it.*

If you are bringing another man to Jesus, you are going to run into all kinds of hindrances.

He hasn't been to church in twenty years. He won't go with you.

He is too strung out on dope to know what's going on. He's not in a condition to go with you.

He's too angry to hear your invitation. Don't try talking to him now.

He's too involved with crime to give it up. Don't endanger yourself.

Tear the roof off! Don't let fear or pride stand in your way. Get that man to Jesus.

I don't know what "roof" separates you or someone you love from Jesus. Whatever it is, it *can* be removed. It can be torn away.

As these men were working on the roof, they were only a matter of feet away from Jesus. They were very close to their miracle. They were not about to be denied.

You are close to your miracle today. Get to Jesus no matter what it takes. Don't let anything stop you.

Don't give up. Jesus has a miracle for you and for those you love. Get to Jesus. His power is sufficient for every need.

Giving a Name to the Fatherless

The Bible doesn't give us the name of the man with palsy. In many Bible stories, we not only have the man's name, but we have his father's name. For example, we know that the blind man in Jericho was Bartimaeus, son of Timaeus. (See Mark 10:46.) When a person's name and father's name are given, the implication is that the person is important. This palsied man was a no-name boy. We don't know his name. We don't know his father. For that matter, he may not have known his own father.

> He said unto the sick of the palsy, Son . . . .
>
> *(Mark 2:5)*

Fathers in the Bible gave their sons status, a place in the society. They gave them their identity. Today — as then — if a boy doesn't have a father, he doesn't have full status. He doesn't have a full identity.

When I look at our society today, I see thousands upon thousands of young men who are fatherless. They group themselves together because they don't belong to a group called family that is led by a leader called father. When I was a boy, my friends and I were afraid to walk into a group of men who might be standing on a street corner. We'd give them a wide berth. Now I see grown men who are afraid to walk into a group of boys. They go out of their way to avoid them.

Fatherless boys are very often called by their problem, not their names. They are labeled just as this man was labeled — "sick of the palsy." He was identified by his condition.

Troublemaker.

Dope-head.

Gang-banger.

Homosexual.

Convict.

Rapist.

Fatherless boys become known for their condition, their predicament, their past actions.

We, as Christians, must go get these fatherless boys. It may take four of us to reach one boy, but we must go get them and bring them to Jesus.

And what did Jesus call this man who was called by everyone else as the one who was "sick of the palsy"? Jesus called him "son." He saw beyond this man's problem and looked into his person. He spoke to him, giving him a name that gave him a relationship. Jesus gave this man an identity, even before He forgave his sins and healed his body!

In calling this man "son," Jesus was taking upon Himself the role of "father." We must do the same.

We must not wait until the fatherless boys we encounter are cleaned up, singing in the choir, or leading the Bible study. Jesus called this young man "son" while he was still sick. He didn't condemn him for what had caused his palsy. He didn't say to this man . . .

You shouldn't have dated that girl.
You shouldn't have hooked up with that gang.
You shouldn't have taken that first drink.
You shouldn't have smoked that first joint.
You shouldn't have gone into that pool hall.
You shouldn't have . . .

No. Jesus loved him as he was. He entered into a relationship with him while he was still sick and in sin.

Neither did Jesus put any qualifications upon His relationship with this man. He didn't say to him . . .

If you'll clean up your life . . .
If you'll agree to do things my way . . .
If you'll stop . . .
If you'll start . . .

No. Jesus loved him without qualification, without condition.

We are called to do the same.

I tell my sons, "You are strong . . . handsome . . . vibrant . . . able . . . resourceful . . . intelligent *men,* not wimps. You are able to take a licking and keep on ticking. You are *somebody!* As God's child, you don't ever have to be lonely, destitute, desperate, or empty. You never have to be jealous of anybody. You are rich soil and fertile ground for a great harvest of blessing."

I have told my daughters repeatedly that I am their first date. I am the one who takes them out to nice places and buys them pretty dresses and shows them a good time. I'm the one who shows them the example of how a man should treat a woman with courtesy and manners. I'm the one who tells them that they are special, beautiful, and lovely in spirit. When they get to be dating age, their dates are going to have a tough act to follow. My daughters are accustomed to affection and praise and kindness; a young man would have a very tough time slapping my daughter and then trying to convince her that she deserved it. She'd likely say to him without any hesitation whatsoever, "I don't *think* so. My daddy told me otherwise."

Tell your children who they are to you, and who they are to God. Do the same for your spiritual sons and daughters.

Every child needs an identity. Every child needs a daddy.

Identify a boy or young man today whom
you can love and help as a spiritual son.
Bring that young man to Christ.
Don't put qualifications, conditions,
or condemnation on him. Love him
as Jesus loves him. Call him "son."

From the Inside Out

Jesus first healed this young palsied man on the inside — down deep where nobody could see any manifestation whatsoever that he had been healed.

So often, we bring a man to Jesus and then we say to ourselves, "Nothing happened." We are looking for signs on the outside. We don't know what Jesus is doing on the inside of that man, or what Jesus has already done to heal him where he hurts the most.

We say, "He doesn't really know Jesus. He's not really saved. If he was saved, he'd . . . ."

We say, "He didn't get delivered. If he was delivered, his life would be cleaned up."

The reality, however, is that God may very well have accomplished a definitive work on the inside of that man. In *God's own timing*, He will also do the outer work.

God heals the man . . . and then He heals the man's marriage.

God saves the soul . . . and then He deals with the man's addiction.

[Jesus said], Why reason ye these things in your hearts? Whether is it easier to say to the sick of the palsy, Thy sins be forgiven thee; or to say, Arise, and take up thy bed, and walk? But that ye may know that the Son of man hath power on earth to forgive sins . . . I say unto thee, Arise, and take up thy bed, and go thy way into thine house.
(Mark 2:8-11)

God delivers the man . . . and then He addresses the issue of the man's finances.

God deals with the inner man . . . and then He gives the promise, delivers the gift, and creates the new identity and reputation.

God doesn't heal our circumstances until He first heals us so we don't destroy the new circumstances He creates!

Believe that God is at work in the ones for whom you are praying . . .

> to whom you are witnessing . . .
>
>> for whom you are believing . . .
>>
>>> and with whom you are ministering.

Believe for both an inner healing and an outer restoration.

**Never dismiss or discount God's ability
to work in ways that may remain
a mystery to you.**

Picking Up
Your Sickbed

Once the Lord has established Himself as Lord over your spirit, He seeks to establish Himself as the Lord over your life. He anoints you, calls you, and leads you into service. He gives you the strength and energy and ability to carry the very thing that once was the mark of your sickness.

Once Jesus had healed this man and raised him up from his sickbed, this man raised up his sickbed and carried it away.

When this palsied man was forgiven and healed by Jesus, he had a bed — but the bed no longer had him.

True deliverance is when you have control over the thing that once controlled you.

You can control your temper, when once your temper ruled you.

You can control your spending habits, when once your lust for things had control over you.

> And immediately he arose, took up the bed, and went forth before them all; insomuch that they were all amazed, and glorified God.
>
> *(Mark 2:12)*

You can control the wandering eye that once was always looking for a new woman to conquer.

Your problem may remain, but it isn't bossing you. It isn't in control of you. You are in control of it.

And to whom does the Lord often call you to minister?

To a person who is in the very condition you were in before you were brought to Jesus! It is to that person that your witness is the most effective because you can say with authority, "I once was lost just like you. But now I am found. I once was blind. But now I see. I once was lying paralyzed and out of control in a sick condition just like you, but now I am healed. Jesus made the difference for me. And He can and will make the difference for you."

**From what has God delivered you?
To whom, then, is He calling you?**

Lift Up Your Hands

I have a young son and when he was learning to walk, he didn't walk with his hands down by his side, but with his hands raised straight up. That position apparently gave him a sense of balance he didn't feel when he had his hands down.

When we raise our hands in praise, we find a new balance for our spiritual lives. We are better able to walk, regardless of the circumstances that may be in our way or which direction our path takes us.

> Thus will I bless thee while I live: I will lift up my hands in thy name.
>
> *(Psalm 63:4)*

No matter how tired I might have been when I got home at night, if my young son came toward me, toddling along with his hands raised up in the air, I couldn't help but pick him up. Even if he was stinky, if he grinned at me with that cute grin of his, I had to pick him up. I'm his father. He's my son. I couldn't help but pick him up and hold him close.

The same for our heavenly Father. He responds to our uplifted hands of praise. He picks us up. He carries us through the places that are too hard for us to walk through. He holds us close and whispers in our ear how much He loves us.

No matter how stinky we may be in our sin, if we will only look toward Him, He picks us up and forgives us. He calls us "son."

You may be wounded . . . but you're still His son.

You may be hurt . . . but you're still His son.

You may be in sin . . . but you're still His son.

He wants to lift you up and heal you so that you can lift up whatever it was that once held you down.

Praise Him today. Lift up your heart, your voice, and your hands to Him.

Reach up today to the One Who is already reaching down to you — your heavenly Father.

About the Author

Born and raised in Charleston, West Virginia, T. D. Jakes has been ministering the Gospel of Jesus Christ for twenty years. In Charleston, he served for sixteen years as Founder and Senior Pastor of Temple of Faith Ministries. In July 1996 Bishop Jakes relocated T. D. Jakes Ministries to Dallas, Texas. There, he is Senior Pastor of The Potter's House, one of the fastest growing churches in the country.

Bishop Jakes' ministry is noted for deep inner healing and practical application of Christian principles amidst the tragedies of life. He is a highly celebrated author of six books including *Woman, Thou Art Loosed!* and *Loose That Man and Let Him Go!*

Bishop Jakes' weekly television program, "Get Ready With T. D. Jakes," airs three times each week on Trinity Broadcasting Network and Black Entertainment Television. The international broadcast reaches numerous countries including the Caribbean, South Africa, and Zimbabwe.

Bishop Jakes resides in Dallas, Texas, with his wife Serita and five children — Jermaine, Jamar, Sara, Cora, and T. D. Jr.

Books by T. D. Jakes

Loose That Man & Let Him Go! Devotional
(Hardcover Gift Edition)

So You Call Yourself a Man!

Lay Aside the Weight

Lay Aside the Weight Workbook & Journal

Woman, Thou Art Loosed! (Hardcover)

Woman, Thou Art Loosed! Devotional

Woman, Thou Art Loosed! Devotional
(Hardcover Gift Edition)

Loose That Man & Let Him Go! (Hardcover)

Loose That Man & Let Him Go! (Softcover)

Loose That Man & Let Him Go! Workbook

T. D. Jakes Speaks to Men!

T. D. Jakes Speaks to Women!

Woman, Thou Art Loosed! (Spanish)

Loose That Man & Let Him Go! (Spanish)

T. D. Jakes Speaks to Men! (Spanish)

T. D. Jakes Speaks to Women! (Spanish)

To contact the Author write:
T. D. Jakes Ministries
P. O. Box 210887
Dallas, Texas 75211

Additional copies of this book and other book titles
from ALBURY PUBLISHING are available
at your local bookstore.

ALBURY PUBLISHING
P. O. Box 470406
Tulsa, Oklahoma 74147-0406
In Canada books are available from:
Word Alive
P. O. Box 670
Niverville, Manitoba
CANADA ROA 1EO